ILLUMINATED
KNITS

LUCY HAGUE

CREDITS

Design, layout & illustration
Lucy Hague

Technical editing & proof-reading
Chaitanya Muralidhara
Fiona Jack

Photography
Tam Ferguson
Lucy Hague

Test-knitters
Fatimah Chang
Charlotte Doesburg
Donna Dupuy
Fiona Jack
Deborah Simon
Beverley Stafford
Karen Steenberg
Frauke Urban

ACKNOWLEDGEMENTS

I'd like to thank all of the people who helped refine and improve the patterns this book: my tech-editor Chaitanya, Fiona and all of my test-knitters. Thank you all for your insightful feedback, suggestions and error-hunting!

Thanks to Cathy and Les at Kathy's Knits, Edinburgh, for all your support and encouragement.

Thank you to Historic Scotland for allowing us access to Inchcolm Abbey, in the Firth of Forth, for our photo shoot, and thanks to Tam for photography assistance!

Finally a big thank-you to my wonderful family, Kath Hague, Keith Hague and Sarah Hague; and to Jamie (for colour advice and everything else!)

Yarn supplied by Malabrigo Yarn.
www.malabrigoyarn.com

Images from the Book of Kells supplied by Bridgeman Art Library and reproduced with permission from Trinity College, Dublin

Second edition, published by Lucy Hague
www.lucyhague.co.uk

CONTENTS

INTRODUCTION

My first book of designs, *Celtic Cable Shawls* (2015), was an attempt
to faithfully translate the interlacing knotwork patterns commonly
found in Insular Celtic art into cable knitting (a particular source of
inspiration for me were the carved Pictish stones, found widely across
Scotland). Before the release of *Celtic Cable Shawls*, I was unsure if the
complexity of the resulting knitting patterns would be too off-putting
for knitters - thankfully the enthusiastic response proved otherwise! I
was very glad to learn that there really is a demand for patterns of this
level of intricacy, and that many knitters are happy to tackle something
complicated as long as the pattern is clearly written and the end result
is worthwhile.

Soon after publishing *Celtic Cable Shawls*, my thoughts started to turn
more to colour. I'd previously experimented with colour-work cables
before, using stranded colour-work knitting, and whilst the finished
results looked good, I personally didn't enjoy the knitting process very
much (I will confess here that my hands are very happy knitting miles
of cables, but they become completely confused and clumsy as soon as
I try to hold more than one strand of yarn at a time!). I was aware of a
particular knitting technique, combining slipped stitches with striping,
that makes seemingly complex colour-work very simple to achieve
with cables, and it only requires you to hold one strand of yarn on each
round. The catch (if it is a catch) is that it can realistically only be used
with designs worked in the round (there are some ways around this,
which I'll mention in the next section).

When I was approached to design a collection for Malabrigo, I realised
that this slipped-stitch cable technique would work excellently with their
intensely vivid and beautifully coloured yarns. Because this technique
requires striping the colours for the background, choosing the colours of
yarn to work with made me think of mixing inks (some colours which
I though would work perfectly together ended up looking muddy, and
others which I thought wouldn't work ended up providing a lovely
contrast to each other). As a source of colour inspiration, I studied the
illuminated Insular manuscripts of the British Isles, created in the early
Celtic Christian period of around 650—800 AD.

BELOW
Detail from the Book of Kells,
fol.188r

ABOVE
Detail from the Book of Kells,
fol.124r, showing decorated
initial 'T'

BELOW
Detail from the Book of Kells,
fol.124r, showing unfinished
knotwork (dotted in red)

In the strictest use of the term, 'illumination' refers to the decoration of a manuscript with precious metals such as gold or silver leaf. Whilst the surviving Insular manuscripts rarely use large amounts of gold or silver, and usually instead rely on pigments such as orpiment (arsenic sulphide) to mimic these precious metals, they can still be described as illuminated. They make use of a creative mixture of limited colours to create a dazzling jewelled effect, and an overall sense of extraordinary richness and complex decoration.

Like all of the finest examples of Insular Celtic art (including the Pictish stones that influenced the designs of my first book), manuscripts such as the Book of Kells perfectly balance a harmonic sense of form with intricate and finely detailed interlacing knotwork, spirals and contorted decorative animal shapes. The pages of these manuscripts seem to be designed to be viewed at different distances - from far away, letters, shapes and portraits of the saints are visible and recognisable, then up close the true complexity of the filled-in spaces reveals itself.

Gerald of Wales wrote in the 12th century of a gospel book he saw at Kildare in Ireland (quite possibly the Book of Kells): "Fine craftsmanship is all about you, but you might not notice it. Look more keenly at it and you will penetrate to the very shrine of art. You will make out intricacies, so delicate and so subtle, so full of knots and links, with colours so fresh and vivid, that you might say that all this were the work of an angel, and not of a man."

In creating the designs for this book, I was strongly influenced by the clever use of pigments by the scribes and artists who created these awe-inspiring manuscripts , and I very much enjoyed the process of combining these colours with complex cables.

I hope that readers of this book will enjoy knitting these designs, as much as I enjoyed creating them, and perhaps even come up with your own unique colour combinations to illuminate your knitting.

SLIPPED-STITCH CABLING

All of the designs in this book use slipped-stitch cabling, worked in the round. This is a simple technique that can create contrasting colour effects. Understanding how this works will help you to plan which colours to use, and how to work the different cable stitches (this technique is essentially the same as mosaic knitting, combined with cable knitting).

Using two different colours of yarn (designated Yarn A and Yarn B), the knitting is worked in single-round stripes, e.g. Round 1 is worked with Yarn A, Round 2 is worked with Yarn B, and so on. When the cable pattern is worked in Yarn A, on the very next round these stitches are slipped, with the working yarn held to the back. This ensures that the

SLIPPED-STITCH CABLES ILLUSTRATED

In the following illustrations, which briefly illustrate the slipped-stitch cable technique, Yarn A is yellow and Yarn B is a variegated turquoise-purple yarn (Malabrigo Sock yarn in *Ochre* and *Indiecita*, respectively).

1 On a Yarn A rnd, all stitches are worked (background stitches are purled and cable stitches are worked as directed).

2 After completing a Yarn A rnd; note that all stitches on the needle are Yarn A.

3 On the next rnd, Yarn B is used to knit the background stitches.

4 When the cable stitches are reached, they are slipped (purlwise), with Yarn B held to the back.

5 After completing a Yarn B rnd; note that all background stitches on the needle are Yarn B, and the cable stitches are Yarn A.

contrasting part of the pattern is only ever worked in Yarn A, and so it appears as a different colour to the background (which appears as a striped mixture of A and B).

One of the interesting benefits of this technique, in addition to it being very easy to work, is that it creates a very neat reverse side to the fabric. Unlike stranded knitting, where floated yarn will be visible, the reverse side looks like normal striped knitted fabric (the working yarn, which is held to the back when stitches are slipped, is only visible if you look very closely). This makes it very useful for working shawls, scarves, blankets and any other item where the reverse side will be seen.

This technique uses a lot of yarn, resulting in a fabric that is surprisingly dense and heavy. This is due to the way that the slipped stitches pull the fabric in vertically, and the way that the cables pull the fabric in horizontally. Gauge is listed in stocking stitch for all the patterns, as I find this is the easiest stitch pattern to swatch, block and measure. However if you're unsure about your gauge I recommend swatching a small part of the cable chart for the pattern you want to knit, and blocking, to check that you like the density and feel of the cabled fabric.

This technique is best worked in the round, over single-round stripes (working the stripes over two rows is possible, but it pulls the fabric in vertically even more, because the stitches which are slipped need to wait two rows, instead of one round, before they are worked again). When working single-round stripes in the round, neither of the yarns have to be broken, because the end of the round is at the same point as the beginning of the round, and so both yarns can be alternately carried up the back of the work at this point.

It is possible, but a bit tricky, to work single-row stripes flat. Imagine working Row 1 in Yarn A, then turning and working Row 2 in Yarn B. When you come to work Row 3 in Yarn A again the yarn will still be at the other end of the work (at the end of Row 1), so it's impossible to carry the yarn without breaking as you would when working in the round.

There are two possible solutions to the problem described above. The first solution is to break the yarn at the end of every row, and join in new yarn at the beginning of every row, which of course leaves a lot of loose ends to weave in later and is rather messy. The second, probably more satisfactory, solution is to work Rows 1 and 2 with the right-side facing, then turn and work Rows 3 and 4 with the wrong-side facing (and then continue working two rows right-side, followed by two rows wrong-side). This allows you to carry the yarn up alternating sides of the work without ever needing to break the yarn.

Generally speaking, the designs in this book would be fairly tricky to convert to flat knitting, because you would need to also convert some of the cable stitches to work on the wrong-side; I wanted to describe the difficulties of translating this technique in flat-knitting to explain the method of working corner sections of the Durrow shawl, where the second solution is used.

There's unfortunately insufficient space to go into further details on the various cable stitches used, which are all explained in the Chart Key & Abbreviations section (p.73). Further information and tutorials are available on my website: **www.lucyhague.co.uk/tutorials**

COMBINING COLOURS

The colour combinations used in the designs in this book were inspired by the pigments used in Insular manuscripts. If you would like to choose your own colour combinations, the following guidelines may be helpful.

First of all, whilst contrast is important to consider, it's not completely essential. Any of these designs could be worked in a single colour, and the cable patterns would still be visible, provided that the colour chosen is not too dark (incidentally, if you do choose to work any of the designs in a single colour, I would recommend still slipping the stitches where directed, to maintain the correct proportions).

If you don't know where to begin, the colour wheel can be a useful starting point. Remember that colours have hue (the colour itself, e.g. green), saturation (e.g. vivid green versus washed-out greyish-green) and luminosity (e.g. dark green versus light green). The colour wheel depicted shows the hues with progressively higher luminosity towards the centre (for saturation, imagine the hues becoming more grey and washed-out towards the centre).

For maximum contrast, pick two colours which oppose each other on the wheel, for example red-orange and blue-green. Sometimes this works well but it can pose the danger of clashing a bit too much. If you choose two opposed colours, it will likely work better if one is more vividly

saturated and the other more washed-out. For a subtler contrast, pick two colours which are separated by one or two segments on the wheel, for example purple and blue-green or yellow-green and orange. Colours chosen in this way can usually work together at a similar level of saturation and luminosity without clashing.

For a very subtle and harmonious contrast, pick two colours which are close in hue, or the same hue, but different in saturation and/or luminosity, for example a vivid dark red-purple with a lighter and/ or greyer red-purple (so, pick a hue on the wheel shown, then move in towards the centre to pick another shade in the same segment).

MAKING A COLOUR SWATCH

It's useful to swatch any combination that you are considering, as it can be surprising how different colours behave together once they are knitted up with slipped-stitch cables. The swatch chart provided can be used for this (as well as for familiarising yourself with slipped-stitch cables before beginning a project).

To make the swatch, cast on 28 sts with Yarn B to a DPN or short circular needle. Without turning, join in Yarn A at beginning of sts just cast-on and work Rnd 1 of Colour Swatch Chart/Written Instructions; without turning, bring Yarn B loosely across back of work to beginning of sts just worked and work Rnd 2 (this method allows you to quickly 'fake' working in the round, i.e. the RS is always facing you).

Continue to work from Chart/Written Instructions, using Yarn A on all odd-numbered rnds and Yarn B on all even-numbered rnds until swatch is desired length. To block swatch, cast-off all sts and cut the yarn that is stranded across the back, so that the swatch can be laid out flat.

COLOUR SWATCH CHART

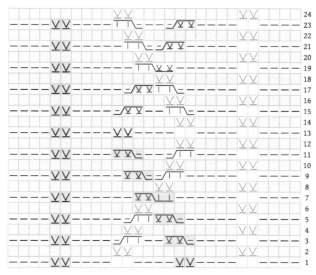

COLOUR SWATCH WRITTEN INSTRUCTIONS

Rnd 1 [Yarn A]: (p4, k2, p4, sl2) 2 times, p4. **28 sts**

Rnd 2 [Yarn B]: k4, (sl2, k10) 2 times.

Rnd 3: p4, k2, p4, T3L{*sl2*}, p2, T3R, p4, sl2, p4.

Rnd 4: k4, sl2, k9, sl2, k11.

Rnd 5: p4, k2, p5, T3L{*sl2*}, T3R, p5, sl2, p4.

Rnd 6: k4, sl2, k8, sl2, k12.

Rnd 7: p4, k2, p6, C4L{*sl2*}, p6, sl2, p4.

Rnd 8: k4, sl2, k6, sl2, k14.

Rnd 9: p4, k2, p5, T3R, T3L{*sl2*}, p5, sl2, p4.

Rnd 10: k4, sl2, k5, sl2, k15.

Rnd 11: p4, k2, p4, T3R, p2, T3L{*sl2*}, p4, sl2, p4.

Rnd 12: (k4, sl2) 2 times, k16.

Rnd 13: (p4, k2) 2 times, (p4, sl2) 2 times, p4.

Rnd 14: repeat Rnd 12.

Rnd 15: p4, k2, p4, T3L, p2, T3R{*sl2*}, p4, sl2, p4.

Rnd 16: repeat Rnd 10.

Rnd 17: p4, k2, p5, T3L, T3R{*sl2*}, p5, sl2, p4.

Rnd 18: repeat Rnd 8.

Rnd 19: p4, k2, p6, C4L[*sl2*]{*k2*}, p6, sl2, p4.

Rnd 20: repeat Rnd 6.

Rnd 21: p4, k2, p5, T3R{*sl2*}, T3L, p5, sl2, p4.

Rnd 22: repeat Rnd 4.

Rnd 23: p4, k2, p4, T3R{*sl2*}, p2, T3L, p4, sl2, p4.

Rnd 24: repeat Rnd 2.

For Chart Key & Abbreviations please see p. 73

RIGHT

Yarn A: *Aguas* (turquoise)
Yarn B: *Botticelli red* (rust red)

COLOUR SWATCH EXAMPLES

All of the swatches on this page have been worked in different shades of Malabrigo Sock (the name of the shade is given, along with a description of the colour).

ABOVE

Yarn A: *Persia* (dark blue-green)
Yarn B: *Turner* (gold-green)

ABOVE

Yarn A: *Indiecita* (variegated turquoise-purple)
Yarn B: *Zarzamora* (dark purple-green)

IONA
Blanket
p. 14

LINDISFARNE
Rectangular shawl
p. 22

DURROW
Triangular shawl
p. 36

KELLS
Pullover
p. 54

IONA

IONA

Inspired by the richly decorated carpet pages of illuminated manuscripts, this blanket is assembled from individual squares, worked separately in the round from the centre out and then attached with a three-needle cast-off (as pictured) or seamed together.

The blanket pictured is made up of 35 squares, arranged 7 × 5, but could easily be modified to be larger or smaller by working more or fewer squares.

MATERIALS
• 3.5 mm/US size 4 DPNs (or needles for preferred method of working small circumferences in the round)
• 3.5 mm/US size 4 long circ needles (optional; for working edging/three-needle cast-off)
• Cable needle
• **Malabrigo Sock Yarn** in the following shades:

  Turner - 2 skeins [774 yds/(702 m)]
  Ochre - 2 skeins [600 yds/(549 m)]
  Archangel - 1 skein [208 yds/(192 m)]
  Rayon Vert - 1 skein [234 yds/(216 m)]
  Aguas - 1 skein [234 yds/(216 m)]

• Waste yarn
• Safety pins
• 1 stitch marker (4 if working optional edging)
• Darning needle

FINISHED MEASUREMENTS
Measurements of 35-square blanket pictured:
28″ × 39″/(71 cm × 99 cm)
• Each square measures approx. 5½″/(14 cm) along each edge after blocking
• Optional blanket edging is approx. ¼″/(0.5 cm) deep

GAUGE
22 sts and 37 rnds over 4″/(10 cm), in stocking stitch after blocking

YARDAGE REQUIREMENTS
For one square:
Yarn A: 30 yds/(27 m)
Yarn B: 26 yds/(24 m)

For Edging (for 35-square blanket):
90 yds/(82 m)

NOTES ON COLOUR CHOICES

Each square requires two different colours: Yarn A, which is used for the cabled pattern and Yarn B, which forms the background. See the section Combining Colours (p. 9) for more information on how to choose and swatch colour combinations.

YARN A: *Ochre* (yellow)
YARN B: *Turner* (green)
9 squares in pictured blanket

PATTERN NOTES

Refer to the Chart Key & Abbreviations section (p. 73) for detailed information regarding elongated stitches.

DIRECTIONS

With Yarn B (background colour), cast on 4 sts to single DPN. At beginning of row, join in Yarn A (cable colour) and pfb 4 times. **8 sts**

YARN A: *Turner* (green)
YARN B: *Aguas* (blue-green)
9 squares in pictured blanket

Arrange sts evenly on DPNs. With Yarn B, pm and join to work in the rnd; k all sts.

With Yarn A, work Rnd 1 of Cable Chart (p. 21)/ Written Instructions (p. 20); with Yarn B, work Rnd 2. Continue to work from Cable Chart/ Written Instructions, using Yarn A on all odd-numbered rnds and Yarn B on all even-numbered rnds. When working with Yarn B, the sts that form the contrasting cable pattern are slipped whenever encountered (slip purlwise with yarn held at back of work). If you find the final M1p of a rnd difficult to work, due to the colour changes, you can substitute a different inc, such as a pfb.

YARN A: *Ochre* (yellow)
YARN B: *Archangel* (pink-orange)
8 squares in pictured blanket

After working Rnd 35 of Cable Chart/Written Instructions, st count is **116 sts.**

If casting off squares and seaming together: cast off all sts, break yarn and weave in ends; block square

YARN A: *Turner* (green)
YARN B: *Rayon Vert* (purple-green)
9 squares in pictured blanket

to approx. 6"/(15 cm) along each side; after drying, the square will contract back to approx. 5½"/(14 cm) along each side.

If joining squares with three-needle cast-off: break Yarn A, leaving a length of approx. 30"/(76 cm), and break Yarn B, leaving a short length to weave in. Cut 4 lengths of waste yarn, each approx. 8"/(20 cm) long. Starting at the beginning of the rnd, using a darning needle, sl 29 sts to one length of waste yarn; repeat with other 3 lengths of waste yarn. Weave in end of Yarn B, and ends at centre of square. Block square to approx. 6"/(15 cm); after drying, the square will contract back to approx. 5½"/(14 cm).

Repeat directions to make as many squares as required (the blanket pictured contains 35 squares).

JOINING SQUARES

Decide on the arrangement of the squares and either sew together the cast-off edges with sewing thread/yarn (if seaming together) or follow the directions on p. 19 (if joining with a three-needle cast-off).

EDGING & FINISHING

Note that if you've chosen to sew the squares together, all edges of the blanket will already be cast-off, and so the Edging is optional; if you wish to add the Edging, pick up and knit the required number of sts evenly across each side of the blanket, then proceed with the Edging instructions, beginning on Set-up Round.

The following directions are given for the three-needle cast-off version, in which live sts are held on lengths of waste yarn on each side of blanket (st counts are given for a 35-square blanket, with squares arranged 5 × 7, as pictured).

With RS facing, beginning at one corner st to the right of a 5-square blanket edge: (sl 149 sts from waste yarn/safety pins to needle, pm, sl next 209 sts from waste yarn/safety pins to needle, pm) twice. **716 sts**

Set-up Round: With RS still facing, join in yarn; (k1, sl m, M1, k across to m whilst working a M1 in each gap between squares, M1, sl m) 4 times. **744 sts**

Cast on 3 sts to right needle and turn work to WS; work i-cord edging on WS as follows:
I-cord edging: *k2, ssk with st from previous row, sl 3 sts wyib from right needle to left needle; repeat from * to work i-cord edging around entire blanket; removing markers as they are encountered.

Graft 3 remaining sts at end of edging to beginning of edging. Weave in all ends and block blanket to finished measurements.

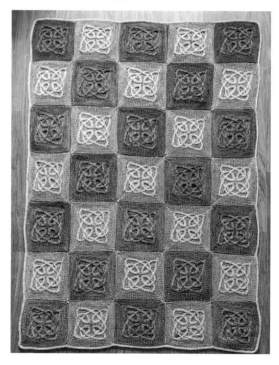

JOINING SQUARES WITH THREE-NEEDLE CAST-OFF

It's important not to cast off too tightly when using this method - you may find it helps to use a DPN one or two sizes larger for your third needle.

Position squares to be joined as shown in Fig. 1 (note position of long tail of Yarn A, indicating end of final rnd). The arrows indicate the edges that will be joined.

On edges to be joined, with RS facing, sl 29 sts from waste yarn to DPN, then sl first st on DPN to safety pin/small stitch holder; **28 sts** on each DPN.

Place squares **with RSs together** and DPNs together; ensure square with long tail at end of sts on DPN is closest to you. With a third DPN, and using long tail, insert needle into each first st on DPNs and k2tog, *insert third DPN into each next st on DPNs and k2tog; pass first st on third DPN over second st and off needle; rep from * until all sts are cast off and 1 st remains on third DPN. Pull yarn up and through rem st; this end will be woven in later.

Repeat instructions to join squares into a strip for the width of the blanket (Fig. 2).

When you have 2 or more strips for the width of the blanket, position strips to be joined as shown in Fig. 3. The arrows indicate the edges that will be joined.

On edges to be joined, with RS facing, sl sts from waste yarn and safety pins to long circs, then sl first st on each circ to safety pin/small stitch holder; **148 sts** on each long circ (for a five-square width blanket).

Place strips **with RSs together** and circs together; with a third DPN, join in yarn and work three-needle cast-off across all sts until all sts are cast off and 1 st remains on third DPN. Pull yarn up and through rem st; weave in end. Note that small gaps may form around the corner joins; use ends from previous lengthwise cast-offs to close up these gaps as you weave them in.

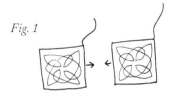

Fig. 1

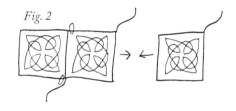

Fig. 2

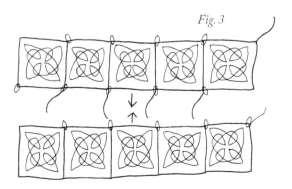

Fig. 3

CABLE CHART WRITTEN INSTRUCTIONS

Rnd 1: (1-into-7, p1) 4 times. **32 sts**

At end of Rnd 1, remove marker, sl 3 sts from beginning of rnd, replace marker.

Rnd 2: (k2, (sl2, k1) twice) 4 times.

Rnd 3: (p1, M1p, (p1, k2) twice, p1, M1p) 4 times. **40 sts**

Rnd 4: (k3, sl2, k1, sl2, k2) 4 times.

Rnd 5: (p3, k2, M1p, p1, M1p, k2, p2) 4 times. **48 sts**

Rnd 6: ((k3, sl2) twice, k2) 4 times.

Rnd 7: (p1, M1p, p2, k2, p3, k2, p2, M1p) 4 times. **56 sts**

Rnd 8: (k4, (sl2, k3) twice) 4 times.

Rnd 9: (p1, M1p, (p3, k2) twice, p3, M1p) 4 times. **64 sts**

Rnd 10: (k5, sl2, k3, sl2, k4) 4 times.

Rnd 11: (1-into-7, p3, T3R, p3, T3L, p3) 4 times. **88 sts**

At end of Rnd 11, remove marker, sl 3 sts from beginning of rnd, replace marker.

Rnd 12: (k2, sl2, k3, sl2, k5, sl2, k3, sl2, k1) 4 times.

Rnd 13: (p1, M1p, p1, T4L[*dbl. el.*], T3R, p5, T3L, T4R[*dbl. el.*], p1, M1p) 4 times. **96 sts**

Rnd 14: (k5, sl4, k7, sl4, k4) 4 times.

Rnd 15: (p1, M1p, p4, C4R, p7, C4R, p4, M1p) 4 times.

Rnd 16: (k6, sl4, k7, sl4, k5) 4 times. **104 sts**

Rnd 17: (p1, M1p, p3, T4R[*el.*], T4L[*el.*], p3, T4R[*el.*], T4L[*dbl. el.*], p3, M1p) 4 times. **112 sts**

Rnd 18: (k5, sl2, k4, C3L{*sl2*}, k1, C3R{*sl2*}, k4, C4L{*sl2*}, k2) 4 times.

Rnd 19: (p1, M1p, p2, T4R[*el.*], p5, C5L, p7, T4L[*dbl. el.*]) 4 times. **116 sts**

At end of Rnd 19, work first 2 p sts of T4L[dbl. el]; whilst 2 k sts are still held on cn, sl marker to RN and sl 2 k sts from cn to LN without working; these 2 sts become the first 2 sts of Rnd 20.

Rnd 20: (C5L{*sl2*}, k1, sl2, k7, sl2, k1, sl2, k9) 4 times.

Rnd 21: (p1, M1p, p2, C5L, p1, p3tog, p1, T4R[*el.*], *p1*, T4L[*dbl. el.*], p7) 4 times. **112 sts**

Rnd 22: (k4, sl2, k1, C3L{*sl2*}, k1, C3R{*sl2*}, k5, sl2, k4, k2tog, k1) 4 times. **108 sts**

Rnd 23: (p2, T4R[*el.*], p2, 5-into-1[p.], p6, T4L[*dbl. el.*], p4) 4 times. **92 sts**

Rnd 24: (k2, sl2, k13, sl2, k4) 4 times.

Rnd 25: (T4R[*el.*], *p13*, T5L[*el.*], *p1*) 4 times.

At end of Rnd 25, remove marker, sl 3 sts from beginning of rnd, replace marker.

Rnd 26: (k17, (sl2, k1) twice) 4 times.

Rnd 27: (p1, M1p, p16, 5-into-1[p.], p1, M1p) 4 times. **84 sts**

Rnd 28: k all sts.

Rnd 29: (p1, M1p, p20, M1p) 4 times. **92 sts**

Rnd 30: k all sts.

Rnd 31: (p1, M1p, p22, M1p) 4 times. **100 sts**

Rnd 32: k all sts.

Rnd 33: (p1, M1p, p24, M1p) 4 times. **108 sts**

Rnd 34: k all sts.

Rnd 35: (p1, M1p, p26, M1p) 4 times. **116 sts**

CABLE CHART

CHART KEY

For full Chart Key &
Abbreviations, see p. 73

CHART NOTES

Repeat each line of the chart 4
times across each rnd.

Note that at ends of **Rnds 1, 11,
19 and 25** the beginning-of-rnd
marker shifts slightly. Refer to the
Cable Chart Written Instructions
on p. 20 for step-by-step
directions for how to move the
marker.

LINDISFARNE

LINDISFARNE

This large rectangular shawl makes use of an innovative circular steeked construction that produces a fringed edge. The complex cables were inspired by the varying weights of Celtic knot interlace often seen in illuminated manuscripts; in the central braid, thinner twisted stitch cables alternate in a contrasting colour to the main cable.

The triangular knots at the edges are a reference to the Lindisfarne manuscript, which gives this shawl its name.

GAUGE

24 sts and 39.5 rnds over 4″/(10 cm), in stocking stitch after blocking

MATERIALS

• 3.0 mm/US size 2.5 long circular needles (or size needed to obtain gauge)
• One 3.0 mm/US size 2.5 DPN (optional; for working i-cord cast-off)
• Cable needle
• **Malabrigo Sock Yarn** in the following shades:

    Marte (Yarn A) - 2 skeins [785 yds/ (718 m)]

    Persia (Yarn B) - 2 skeins [640 yds/ (585 m)]

• Waste yarn (optional; for provisional cast-on)
• 3 stitch markers

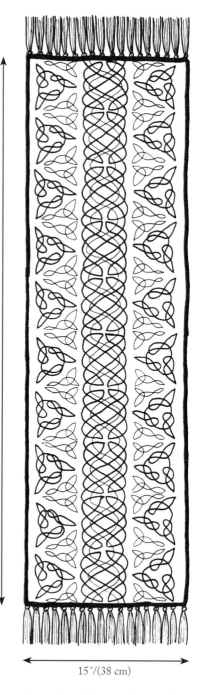

62″(157.5 cm)

15″(38 cm)

Fringe on pictured sample is 4.5″/(11.5 cm) long at each end, after knotting and trimming

ILLUMINATED KNITS | *Lucy Hague*

PATTERN NOTES

This shawl is worked in the round, from one side to the other. A 28-stitch-wide steek (a section of plain knitting) is included, which is cut down the centre after completing the work, and unravelled to form the fringe at each end of the shawl. The width of the steek (14 sts on each side of the beginning of round marker) produces a fringe that is approx. 7″/(18 cm) long at each end; in the sample picture, the fringe has been knotted with 10 strands of yarn in each knot, and then trimmed down to approx. 4.5″/(11.5 cm). The number of steek stitches can be altered to produce a longer or shorter fringe - however, it's important to allow a little extra length, so that the fringe can be neatly trimmed down to a uniform length.

In this pattern, Yarn A is used for the main cable pattern, and Yarn B is used for the thinner twisted-stitch cable pattern. Yarn A and Yarn B are striped on alternate rounds. Most of the cabling occurs on odd-numbered rounds. See the section Combining Colours (p. 9) for more information on how to choose and swatch colour combinations.

Refer to the Chart Key & Abbreviations section (p. 73) for detailed information regarding elongated stitches.

Note that the stitch counts given in the Chart Written Instructions are only for the section contained between the second and third markers (i.e., these stitch counts don't include the steek stitches and the p1tbl on each side of the steek).

DIRECTIONS

Using waste yarn and Yarn B, cast on 375 sts using provisional cast-on; pm and join in Yarn A.
Rnd 1: with Yarn A, k14, p1tbl, pm, k2, p to last 17 sts, k2, pm, p1tbl, k14.
Rnd: 2: join to work in the round with Yarn B, k14, p1tbl, sl2, k to 2 sts before m, sl2, p1tbl, k14.

Work Rnds 1 and 2 a further 2 times (ignoring reference to placing markers); henceforth these 2 rnds are referred to as '*working even in garter st pattern.*'

Rnd 7: with Yarn A, k14, p1tbl, work Rnd 1 of Chart A (p. 27)/Chart A Written Instructions (p. 26), p1tbl, k14.
Rnd 8: with Yarn B, k14, p1tbl, work Rnd 2 of Chart A/Chart A Written Instructions, p1tbl, k14.

Continue to work as set until Chart A is completed.

Work even in garter st pattern for 4 rnds.

Work Chart B (p. 30)/Chart B Written Instructions (p. 29), continuing steek pattern as set.

Work even in garter st pattern for 4 rnds.

Work Chart C (p. 34)/Chart C Written Instructions (p. 32), continuing steek pattern as set.

Work even in garter st pattern for 6 rnds.

I-CORD CAST-OFF
When working i-cord cast-off, remove markers whenever they are encountered; note that the i-cord cast-off begins and ends at the p1tbl on each side of the steek, but is not worked over the steek itself.

Next row: with Yarn A, k14, p1tbl, turn work;
[WS]: sl1, p14, remove marker, p14, k1tbl, turn work;
[RS]: sl1, k28, then with DPN work i-cord cast-off as follows: *k2, ssk, sl 3 sts from DPN back to ln; rep

from * until last marker is reached; then with ln, pass second st then third st over first st on DPN; sl rem st back to ln and work ssk.

Break yarn leaving tail of approx 7″/(18 cm), pull through remaining st on DPN. Sl 28 rem sts to waste yarn/stitch holder.

Turn work upside down; beginning at end of provisional cast-on, undo provisional cast-on and sl 375 sts from waste yarn to circ needle (note that there may be 1 st missing, depending on how the cast-on is undone; check that there are 28 sts in total in the steek section, and make an extra st to compensate if necessary).

Join in Yarn A.
Next row: With Yarn A, k14, p1tbl, turn work;
[WS]: sl1, p28, k1tbl, turn work;
[RS]: sl1, k28, then with DPN, work i-cord cast-off as previously instructed, until base of p1tbl is reached; then with ln, pass second st then third st over first st on DPN; sl rem st back to ln and work ssk. Break yarn leaving tail of approx 7″/(18 cm), pull through remaining st on DPN.

FINISHING

Remove 28 sts from waste yarn/stitch holder, and with a sharp pair of scissors carefully cut along the centre of the steek section (previously marked by the beginning-of-rnd marker). Starting from the top of the steek, very carefully pull each strand out so that the knitted stitches unravel (leaving the p1tbl column intact on each side). Pull out one strand at a time and check it has been fully unravelled before proceeding to the next strand, to avoid tangling.

When all strands have been fully unravelled on both sides, soak shawl in lukewarm water. Carefully press dry in a towel and lay out flat; block to finished measurements and smooth out fringe so that it dries straight.

When shawl is completely dry, knot fringe at regular intervals using overhand knots (sample pictured shows knots of 10 strands each) and then trim fringe to a uniform length (sample pictured shows fringe trimmed down to approx. 4.5″/(11.5 cm).

CHART A WRITTEN INSTRUCTIONS

Rnd 1: k2, (p4, 1-into-5, p25, 1-into-5, p3) 10 times, p1, k2. **425 sts [42 sts in each repeat]**
Rnd 2: sl2, (k1, 1-into-3, k2, sl2, k1, M1, sl2, k25, sl2, M1, k1, sl2, k2, 1-into-3) 10 times, k1, sl2. **485 sts [48 sts in each repeat]**
Rnd 3: k2, (p1, sl1, p1, T2L{*sl1*}, p1, T3L, p1, T4L[*dbl. el.*], p21, T4R[*dbl. el.*], p1, T3R, p1, T2R{*sl1*}, p1, sl1) 10 times, p1, k2.
Rnd 4: sl2, (k1, (k1 tbl, k2) twice, sl2, k3, C4L{*sl2*}, k17, C4R{*sl2*}, k3, sl2, (k2, k1 tbl) twice) 10 times, k1, sl2.
Rnd 5: k2, (p1, sl1, p2, T2L{*sl1*}, p1, T3L, p4, T4L[*dbl. el.*], p3, 1-into-5, p5, 1-into-5, p3, T4R[*dbl. el.*], p4, T3R, p1, T2R{*sl1*}, p2, sl1) 10 times, p1, k2. **565 sts [56 sts in each repeat]**

CHART NOTES

Repeat section in blue border 10 times across each rnd.

CHART KEY

For full Chart Key &
Abbreviations, see p. 73

CHART A

LINDISFARNE

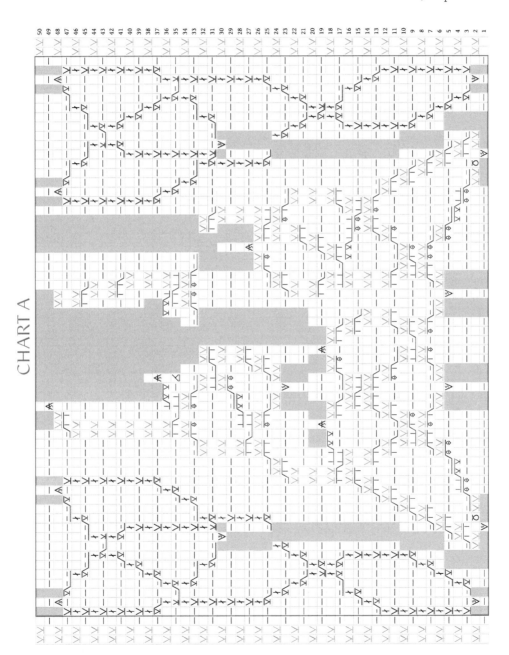

Rnd 6: sl2, (k1, k1 tbl, k3, k1 tbl, k2, sl2, k6, sl2, k3, sl2, k1, sl2, k5, sl2, k1, sl2, k3, sl2, k6, sl2, k2, k1 tbl, k3, k1 tbl) 10 times, k1, sl2.

Rnd 7: k2, (p1, sl1, p3, T2L{*sl1*}, p1, T3L, p5, T4L[*dbl. el.*], T3R, p1, T4L[*el.*], *p1*, T4R[*el.*], *p1*, T4L[*el.*], T3R, p5, T3R, p1, T2R{*sl1*}, p3, sl1) 10 times, p1, k2.

Rnd 8: sl2, (k1, k1 tbl, k4, k1 tbl, k2, sl2, k7, sl4, k4, sl2, k1, sl2, k5, sl4, k6, sl2, k2, k1 tbl, k4, k1 tbl) 10 times, k1, sl2.

Rnd 9: k2, (p1, sl1, p4, T2L{*sl1*}, p1, T3L, p6, C4R[*el.*], p4, C5R, p5, C4R[*el.*], p5, T3R, p1, T2R{*sl1*}, p4, sl1) 10 times, p1, k2.

Rnd 10: sl2, (k1, k1 tbl, k5, k1 tbl, k2, sl2, k6, sl4, k4, sl2, k1, sl2, k5, sl4, k5, sl2, k2, k1 tbl, k5, k1 tbl) 10 times, k1, sl2.

Rnd 11: k2, (p1, sl1, p5, sl1, p2, T3L, p3, T4R[*el.*], T3L, p2, T3R, p1, T4L[*el.*], p2, T3R, T3L, p3, T3R, p2, sl1, p5, sl1) 10 times, p1, k2.

Rnd 12: sl2, (k1, k1 tbl, k5, k1 tbl, (k3, sl2) 3 times, k2, sl2, k4, (sl2, k2) twice, (sl2, k3) twice, k1 tbl, k5, k1 tbl) 10 times, k1, sl2.

Rnd 13: k2, (p1, T2L{*sl1*}, p4, sl1, p3, T4L[*el.*], T3R, p3, k2, p2, k2, p4, T3L, T3R, p2, T3L, p1, T3R, p3, sl1, p4, T2R{*sl1*}) 10 times, p1, k2.

Rnd 14: sl2, (k2, k1 tbl, k4, k1 tbl, k5, sl4, k4, sl2, k2, sl2, k5, sl4, k4, sl2, k1, sl2, (k4, k1 tbl) twice, k1) 10 times, k1, sl2.

Rnd 15: k2, (p2, T2L{*sl1*}, p3, sl1, p5, C4L[*dbl. el.*], p4, k2, p2, T3L, p4, C4L, p4, k2, T3R, p4, sl1, p3, T2R{*sl1*}, p1) 10 times, p1, k2.

Rnd 16: sl2, ((k3, k1 tbl) twice, k5, sl2, C5L{*sl2*}, k1, sl2, k3, sl2, (k4, sl4) twice, k5, k1 tbl, k3, k1 tbl, k2) 10 times, k1, sl2.

Rnd 17: k2, (p3, T3L{*sl1*}, T2R{*sl1*}, p4, T3R, p3, C5R, p3, T3L, p1, T4R[*el.*], T3L,

p3, C4L, p5, T2L{*sl1*}, T3R{*sl1*}, p2) 10 times, p1, k2.

Rnd 18: sl2, (k5, k2tbl, k5, (sl2, k4, sl2, k1) twice, sl2, k3, sl2, k1, C4R{*sl2*}, sl2, k6, k2tbl, k4) 10 times, k1, sl2.

Rnd 19: k2, (p5, C2L{*sl2*}, p5, k2, p3, T3R, p1, T3L, (p3, 5-into-1[*p*]) twice, p2, k2, p6, C2R{*sl2*}, p4) 10 times, p1, k2. **485 sts [48 sts in each repeat]**

Rnd 20: sl2, (k5, k2tbl, k5, (sl2, k3) twice, sl2, k10, sl2, k6, k2tbl, k4) 10 times, k1, sl2.

Rnd 21: k2, (p4, T2R{*sl1*}, T2L{*sl1*}, p4, k2, p2, T3R, p3, k2, p10, k2, p5, T2R{*sl1*}, T2L{*sl1*}, p3) 10 times, p1, k2.

Rnd 22: sl2, (k4, k1 tbl, k2, k1 tbl, k4, sl2, k2, sl2, k4, sl2, k10, sl2, k5, k1 tbl, k2, k1 tbl, k3) 10 times, k1, sl2.

Rnd 23: k2, (p3, T2R{*sl1*}, p2, T2L{*sl1*}, p3, T4L[*el.*], k2, p3, T3R, p3, 1-into-5, p5, T3R, p4, T2R{*sl1*}, p2, T2L{*sl1*}, p2) 10 times, p1, k2. **525 sts [52 sts in each repeat]**

Rnd 24: sl2, (k3, k1 tbl, k4, k1 tbl, k5, sl4, k3, sl2, k4, sl2, k1, (sl2, k5) twice, k1 tbl, k4, k1 tbl, k2) 10 times, k1, sl2.

Rnd 25: k2, (p2, T2R{*sl1*}, p4, T2L{*sl1*}, p4, C4L, p1, T4R[*el.*], p3, T3R, p1, T4L[*el.*], *p1*, T4R, p4, T2R{*sl1*}, p4, T2L{*sl1*}, p1) 10 times, p1, k2.

Rnd 26: sl2, (k2, k1 tbl, k6, k1 tbl, k4, sl4, k1, sl2, k5, sl2, k4, sl2, k1, sl2, (k6, k1 tbl) twice, k1) 10 times, k1, sl2.

Rnd 27: k2, (p2, sl1, p6, sl1, p4, k2, 5-into-1[*p*], p4, T3R, p4, C5L, (p6, sl1) twice, p1) 10 times, p1, k2. **485 sts [48 sts in each repeat]**

Rnd 28: sl2, (k2, k1 tbl, k6, k1 tbl, k4, sl2, k5, sl2, k3, C4R{*sl2*}, k1, sl2, (k6, k1 tbl) twice, k1) 10 times, k1, sl2.

Rnd 29: k2, (p2, sl1, p6, sl1, p4, k2, p5, k2, p1, T4R[*dbl. el.*], p3, k2, (p6, sl1) twice, p1) 10 times, p1, k2.

Rnd 30: sl2, (k2, k1 tbl, k5, 1-into-3, k1 tbl, k4, sl2, k5, sl2, k1, sl2, k5, sl2, k6, k1 tbl, 1-into-3, k5, k1 tbl, k1) 10 times, k1, sl2.

525 sts [52 sts in each repeat]

Rnd 31: k2, (p2, sl1, p3, T3R{*sl1*}, p1, C2L{*sl2*}, p4, T3L, p4, C5R, p5, k2, p6, C2R{*sl2*}, p1, T3L{*sl1*}, p3, sl1, p1) 10 times, p1, k2.

Rnd 32: sl2, (k2, (k1 tbl, k3) twice, k2tbl, k5, sl2, k4, sl2, k1, (sl2, k5) twice, k1, k1tbl, (k1 tbl, k3) twice, k1 tbl, k1) 10 times, k1, sl2.

Rnd 33: k2, (p2, sl1, p1, T3R{*sl1*}, p3, sl1, T3L{*sl1*}, p3, T4L[*el.*], T4R[*el.*], *p1*, T4L[*el.*], *p1*, T4R[*el.*], p4, T3R{*sl1*}, sl1, p3, T3L{*sl1*}, p1, sl1, p1) 10 times, p1, k2.

Rnd 34: sl2, (k2, k1 tbl, k1, k1 tbl, k5, k1 tbl, k2, k1 tbl, k5, sl4, k5, sl2, k1, sl2, k6, k1 tbl, k2, k1 tbl, k5, (k1 tbl, k1) twice) 10 times, k1, sl2.

Rnd 35: k2, (p2, C3L[*sl1, p1, sl1*], p5, sl1, p2, T2L{*sl1*}, p4, C4L, p1, p3 tog, p1, C5L, p5, T2R{*sl1*}, p2, sl1, p5, C3R[*sl1, p1, sl1*], p1) 10 times, p1, k2. **505 sts [50 sts in each repeat]**

Rnd 36: sl2, (k2, k1 tbl, k1, k1 tbl, k5, k1 tbl, k3, k1 tbl, k4, sl2, C3L{*sl2*}, k1, C3R{*sl2*}, k1, sl2, k5, k1 tbl, k3, k1 tbl, k5, (k1 tbl, k1) twice) 10 times, k1, sl2.

Rnd 37: k2, (p1, T2R{*sl1*}, p1, T2L{*sl1*}, p4, sl1, p3, T2L{*sl1*}, p3, k2, p1, 5-into-1[*p*], p2, k2, p4, T2R{*sl1*}, p3, sl1, p4, T2R{*sl1*}, p1, T2L{*sl1*}) 10 times, p1, k2. **465 sts [46 sts in each repeat]**

Rnd 38: sl2, (k1, k1 tbl, k3, (k1 tbl, k4) twice, k1 tbl, k3, sl2, k4, sl2, (k4, k1 tbl) 3 times, k3, k1 tbl) 10 times, k1, sl2.

Rnd 39: k2, (p1, sl1, p3, T2L{*sl1*}, p3, sl1, p4, sl1, p3, (k2, p4) twice, sl1, p4, sl1, p3, T2R{*sl1*}, p3, sl1) 10 times, p1, k2.

Rnd 40: sl2, (k1, (k1 tbl, k4, k1 tbl, k3) twice, (sl2, k4) twice, k1 tbl, k4, k1 tbl, k3, k1 tbl, k4, k1 tbl) 10 times, k1, sl2.

Rnd 41: k2, (p1, sl1, p4, T2L{*sl1*}, p1, T2R{*sl1*}, p4, sl1, p3, T3L, p3, k2, p4, sl1, p4, T2L{*sl1*}, p1, T2R{*sl1*}, p4, sl1) 10 times, p1, k2.

Rnd 42: sl2, ((k, k1 tbl, k5, k1 tbl) twice, k4, sl2, k3, sl2, k4, k1 tbl, k5, k1 tbl, k1, k1 tbl, k5, k1 tbl) 10 times, k1, sl2.

Rnd 43: k2, (p1, sl1, p5, C3R[*sl1, p1, sl1*], p5, sl1, p4, k2, p3, k2, p4, sl1, p5, C3L[*sl1, p1, sl1*], p5, sl1) 10 times, p1, k2.

Rnd 44: repeat Rnd 42.

Rnd 45: k2, (p1, sl1, p3, T3R{*sl1*}, p1, T3L{*sl1*}, p3, sl1, p4, T3L, p2, k2, p4, sl1, p3, T3R{*sl1*}, p1, T3L{*sl1*}, p3, sl1) 10 times, p1, k2.

Rnd 46: sl2, (k1, (k1 tbl, k3, k1 tbl, k5) twice, sl2, k2, sl2, k4, k1 tbl, k3, k1 tbl, k5, k1 tbl, k3, k1 tbl) 10 times, k1, sl2.

Rnd 47: k2, (p1, sl1, p1, T3R{*sl1*}, p5, T3L{*sl1*}, p1, sl1, p5, k2, p1, T3R, p4, sl1, p1, T3R{*sl1*}, p5, T3L{*sl1*}, p1, sl1) 10 times, p1, k2.

Rnd 48: sl2, (k1, 3-into-1, k9, 3-into-1, k5, sl2, k1, sl2, k5, 3-into-1, k9, 3-into-1) 10 times, k1, sl2. **385 sts [38 sts in each repeat]**

Rnd 49: k2, (p17, 5-into-1[*p*], p16) 10 times, p1, k2. **345 sts [34 sts in each repeat]**

Rnd 50: sl2, k341, sl2.

CHART B WRITTEN INSTRUCTIONS

Rnd 1: (On first repeat only, work kfbf instead of first 1-into-5); k2, (1-into-5, p8,

CHART NOTES

Repeat section in blue border 10 times across each rnd.

In Chart B, for turquoise squares on Rnds 1, 8, 38 and 45, work a kfbf, kfb, k2tog and k3tog, respectively, *on the first repeat only.*

CHART B

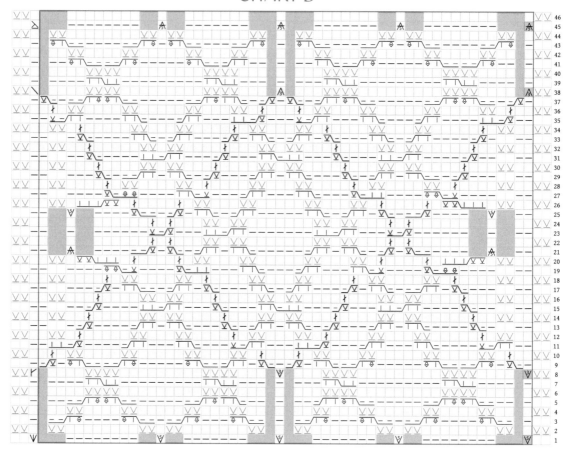

ILLUMINATED KNITS | *Lucy Hague*

(1-into-5, p7) twice, 1-into-5, p8) 10 times, kfbf, k2. **505 sts [50 sts in each repeat]**

Rnd 2: sl2, (k1, sl2, k8, (sl2, k1, sl2, k7) twice, sl2, k1, sl2, k8, sl2) 10 times, k1, sl2.

Rnd 3: k2, (p1, T4L[*el.*], p4, (T4R[*el.*], *p1*, T4L[*el.*], p3) twice, T4R[*el.*], *p1*, T4L[*el.*], p4, T4R[*el.*]) 10 times, p1, k2.

Rnd 4: sl2, (k3, sl2, k4, (sl2, k5, sl2, k3) twice, sl2, k5, sl2, k4, sl2, k2) 10 times, k1, sl2.

Rnd 5: k2, (p3, T4L[*el.*], T4R[*el.*], p5, T4L[*el.*], T3R, p5, T3L, T4R[*el.*], p5, T4L[*el.*], T4R[*el.*], p2) 10 times, p1, k2.

Rnd 6: sl2, (k5, sl4, k9, sl4, k7, sl4, k9, sl4, k4) 10 times, k1, sl2.

Rnd 7: k2, (p5, C4L, p9, C4L, p7, C4L, p9, C4L, p4) 10 times, p1, k2.

Rnd 8: (On first repeat only, work kfb instead of first 1-into-3); sl2, (1-into-3, k4, sl4, k9, sl4, k3, 1-into-3, k3, sl4, k9, sl4, k4) 10 times, kfb, sl2. **545 sts [54 sts in each repeat]**

Rnd 9: k2, (p1, T2L{*sl1*}, p1, T4R[*el.*], T4L[*el.*], p5, T4R[*el.*], T3L, p1, T2R{*sl1*}, p1, T2L{*sl1*}, p1, T3R, T4L[*el.*], p5, T4R[*el.*], T4L[*el.*], *p1*, T2R{*sl1*}) 10 times, p1, k2.

Rnd 10: sl2, (k2, k1 tbl, k1, sl2, k4, sl2, k5, sl2, k3, sl2, k1, k1 tbl, k3, k1 tbl, k1, sl2, k3, sl2, k5, sl2, k4, sl2, k1, k1 tbl, k1) 10 times, k1, sl2.

Rnd 11: k2, (p2, C4R[*T2L{sl1}*], p4, T3L, p3, T3R, p3, C4R{*sl1*}[T3L], p3, C4R[*T2L{sl1}*], p3, T3L, p3, T3R, p4, C4R{*sl1*}[T3L], p1) 10 times, p1, k2.

Rnd 12: sl2, (k2, sl2, k1, k1 tbl, k5, sl2, k3, sl2, k4, k1 tbl, k1, sl2, k3, sl2, k1, k1 tbl, k4, sl2, k3, sl2, k5, k1 tbl, k1, sl2, k1) 10 times, k1, sl2.

Rnd 13: k2, (p2, k2, p1, T2L{*sl1*}, p4, T3L, p1, T3R, p3, T2R{*sl1*}, p1, T3L, p1, T3R, p1,

T2L{*sl1*}, p3, T3L, p1, T3R, p4, T2R{*sl1*}, p1, k2, p1) 10 times, p1, k2.

Rnd 14: sl2, (k2, sl2, k2, k1 tbl, k5, sl2, k1, sl2, k4, k1 tbl, k3, sl2, k1, sl2, k3, k1 tbl, k4, sl2, k1, sl2, k5, k1 tbl, k2, sl2, k1) 10 times, k1, sl2.

Rnd 15: k2, (p2, k2, p2, T2L{*sl1*}, p4, C5R, p3, T2R{*sl1*}, p3, C5L, p3, T2L{*sl1*}, p3, C5R, p4, T2R{*sl1*}, p2, k2, p1) 10 times, p1, k2.

Rnd 16: sl2, (k2, (sl2, k3, k1 tbl, k4, sl2, k1) twice, (sl2, k4, k1 tbl, k3, sl2, k1) twice) 10 times, k1, sl2.

Rnd 17: k2, (p2, k2, p3, T2L{*sl1*}, p1, T4R, p1, T3L, p1, T2R{*sl1*}, p3, T3R, p1, T3L, p3, T2L{*sl1*}, p1, T3R, p1, T4L, p1, T2R{*sl1*}, p3, k2, p1) 10 times, p1, k2.

Rnd 18: sl2, (k2, sl2, k4, k1 tbl, k1, sl2, k4, sl2, k1, k1 tbl, k4, sl2, k3, sl2, k4, k1 tbl, k1, sl2, k4, sl2, k1, k1 tbl, k4, sl2, k1) 10 times, k1, sl2.

Rnd 19: k2, (p2, k2, p4, C4L{*sl1*}[T3R{dbl. el.}], p4, C4L[*T2R{sl1}*], p3, T3R, p3, T3L, p3, C4L{*sl1*}[T3R], p4, C4L{dbl. el.}[*T2R{sl1}*], p4, k2, p1) 10 times, p1, k2.

Rnd 20: sl2, (k2, sl2, k1, C5R{*sl2*}, k1, k1 tbl, k4, k1 tbl, k1, sl2, k3, sl2, k5, sl2, k3, sl2, k1, k1 tbl, k4, k1 tbl, k1, C5L{*sl2*}, k1, sl2, k1) 10 times, k1, sl2.

Rnd 21: k2, (p2, 5-into-1[*p*], p4, T3L{*sl1*}, p1, T2R{*sl1*}, p1, T3L, p1, T3R, p5, T3L, p1, T3R, p1, T2L{*sl1*}, p1, T3R{*sl1*}, p4, 5-into-1[*p*], p1) 10 times, p1, k2. **465 sts [46 sts in each repeat]**

Rnd 22: sl2, (k9, k1 tbl, k1, k1 tbl, k3, sl2, k1, sl2, k7, sl2, k1, sl2, k3, k1 tbl, k1, k1 tbl, k8) 10 times, k1, sl2.

Rnd 23: k2, (p9, C3R[*sl1, p1, sl1*], p3, C5R, p7, C5R, p3, C3R[*sl1, p1, sl1*], p8) 10 times, p1, k2.

Rnd 24: repeat Rnd 22.

Rnd 25: k2, (p2, 1-into-5, p4, T3R{*sl1*}, p1, T2L{*sl1*}, p1, T3R, p1, T3L, p5, T3R, p1, T3L, p1, T2R{*sl1*}, p1, T3L{*sl1*}, p4, 1-into-5, p1) 10 times, p1, k2. **545 sts [54 sts in each repeat]**

Rnd 26: sl2, (k2, sl2, k1, C5L{*sl2*}, k1, k1 tbl, k4, k1 tbl, k1, sl2, k3, sl2, k5, sl2, k3, sl2, k1, k1 tbl, k4, k1 tbl, k1, C5R{*sl2*}, k1, sl2, k1) 10 times, k1, sl2.

Rnd 27: k2, (p2, k2, p4, C4L{dbl. el.} [T2R{*sl1*}], p4, C4L{*sl1*}[T3R], p3, T3L, p3, T3R, p3, C4L[*T2R{sl1}*], p4, C4L{*sl1*} [T3R{dbl. el.}], p4, k2, p1) 10 times, p1, k2.

Rnd 28: repeat Rnd 18.

Rnd 29: k2, (p2, k2, p3, T2R{*sl1*}, p1, T4L, p1, T3R, p1, T2L{*sl1*}, p3, T3L, p1, T3R, p3, T2R{*sl1*}, p1, T3L, p1, T4R, p1, T2L{*sl1*}, p3, k2, p1) 10 times, p1, k2.

Rnd 30: repeat Rnd 16.

Rnd 31: k2, (p2, k2, p2, T2R{*sl1*}, p4, C5R, p3, T2L{*sl1*}, p3, C5L, p3, T2R{*sl1*}, p3, C5R, p4, T2L{*sl1*}, p2, k2, p1) 10 times, p1, k2.

Rnd 32: repeat Rnd 14.

Rnd 33: k2, (p2, k2, p1, T2R{*sl1*}, p4, T3R, p1, T3L, p3, T2L{*sl1*}, p1, T3R, p1, T3L, p1, T2R{*sl1*}, p3, T3R, p1, T3L, p4, T2L{*sl1*}, p1, k2, p1) 10 times, p1, k2.

Rnd 34: sl2, (k2, sl2, k1, k1 tbl, k5, sl2, k3, sl2, k4, k1 tbl, k1, sl2, k3, sl2, k1, k1 tbl, k4, sl2, k3, sl2, k5, k1 tbl, k1, sl2, k1) 10 times, k1, sl2.

Rnd 35: k2, (p2, C4R{*sl1*}[T3L], p4, T3R, p3, T3L, p3, C4R[*T2L{sl1}*], p3, C4R{*sl1*}[T3L], p3, T3R, p3, T3L, p4, C4R[*T2L{sl1}*], p1) 10 times, p1, k2.

Rnd 36: repeat Rnd 10.

Rnd 37: k2, (p1, T2R{*sl1*}, p1, T4L[*el.*],

T4R[*el.*], p5, T4L[*el.*], T3R, p1, T2L{*sl1*}, p1, T2R{*sl1*}, p1, T3L, T4R[*el.*], p5, T4L[*el.*], T4R[*el.*], *p1*, T2L{*sl1*}) 10 times, p1, k2.

Rnd 38: (On first repeat only, work k2tog instead of first 3-into-1); sl2, (3-into-1, k4, sl4, k9, sl4, k3, 3-into-1, k3, sl4, k9, sl4, k4) 10 times, ssk, sl2. **505 sts [50 sts in each repeat]**

Rnd 39: repeat Rnd 7.

Rnd 40: repeat Rnd 6.

Rnd 41: k2, (p3, T4R[*el.*], T4L[*el.*], p5, T4R[*el.*], T3L, p5, T3R, T4L[*el.*], p5, T4R[*el.*], T4L[*el.*], p2) 10 times, p1, k2.

Rnd 42: sl2, (k3, sl2, k4, (sl2, k5, sl2, k3) twice, sl2, k5, sl2, k4, sl2, k2) 10 times, k1, sl2.

Rnd 43: k2, (p1, T4R[*el.*], p4, (T4L[*el.*], *p1*, T4R[*el.*], p3) twice, T4L[*el.*], *p1*, T4R[*el.*], p4, T4L[*el.*]) 10 times, p1, k2.

Rnd 44: repeat Rnd 2.

Rnd 45: (On first repeat only, work k3tog instead of first 5-into-1[p.]); k2, (5-into-1[*p*], p8, (5-into-1[*p*], p7) twice, 5-into-1[*p*], p8) 10 times, sssp, k2. **345 sts [34 sts in each repeat]**

Rnd 46: sl2, k341, sl2.

CHART C WRITTEN INSTRUCTIONS

Rnd 1: k2, (p17, 1-into-5, p16) 10 times, p1, k2. **385 sts [38 sts in each repeat]**

Rnd 2: sl2, (k1, 1-into-3, k9, 1-into-3, k5, sl2, k1, sl2, k5, 1-into-3, k9, 1-into-3) 10 times, k1, sl2. **465 sts [46 sts in each repeat]**

Rnd 3: k2, (p1, sl1, p1, T3L{*sl1*}, p5, T3R{*sl1*}, p1, sl1, p4, T3R, p1, k2, p5, sl1, p1, T3L{*sl1*}, p5, T3R{*sl1*}, p1, sl1) 10 times, p1, k2.

Rnd 4: sl2, (k1, k1 tbl, k3, k1 tbl, k5, k1 tbl, k3, k1 tbl, k4, sl2, k2, sl2, (k5, k1 tbl, k3, k1 tbl) twice) 10 times, k1, sl2.

Rnd 5: k2, (p1, sl1, p3, T3L{*sl1*}, p1, T3R{*sl1*}, p3, sl1, p4, k2, p2, T3L, p4, sl1, p3, T3L{*sl1*}, p1, T3R{*sl1*}, p3, sl1) 10 times, p1, k2.

Rnd 6: sl2, ((k, k1 tbl, k5, k1 tbl) twice, k4, sl2, k3, sl2, k4, k1 tbl, k5, k1 tbl, k1, k1 tbl, k5, k1 tbl) 10 times, k1, sl2.

Rnd 7: k2, (p1, sl1, p5, C3L[*sl1, p1, sl1*], p5, sl1, p4, k2, p3, k2, p4, sl1, p5, C3R[*sl1, p1, sl1*], p5, sl1) 10 times, p1, k2.

Rnd 8: repeat Rnd 6.

Rnd 9: k2, (p1, sl1, p4, T2R{*sl1*}, p1, T2L{*sl1*}, p4, sl1, p4, k2, p3, T3L, p3, sl1, p4, T2R{*sl1*}, p1, T2L{*sl1*}, p4, sl1) 10 times, p1, k2.

Rnd 10: sl2, (k1, k1 tbl, k4, k1 tbl, k3, (k1 tbl, k4) twice, sl2, k4, sl2, (k3, k1 tbl, k4, k1 tbl) twice) 10 times, k1, sl2.

Rnd 11: k2, (p1, sl1, p3, T2R{*sl1*}, p3, (sl1, p4) twice, k2, p4, k2, p3, sl1, p4, sl1, p3, T2L{*sl1*}, p3, sl1) 10 times, p1, k2.

Rnd 12: sl2, (k1, k1 tbl, k3, (k1 tbl, k4) 3 times, sl2, k4, sl2, k3, (k1 tbl, k4) twice, k1 tbl, k3, k1 tbl) 10 times, k1, sl2.

Rnd 13: k2, (p1, T2L{*sl1*}, p1, T2R{*sl1*}, p4, sl1, p3, T2R{*sl1*}, p4, k2, p2, 1-into-5, p1, k2, p3, T2L{*sl1*}, p3, sl1, p4, T2L{*sl1*}, p1, T2R{*sl1*}) 10 times, p1, k2. **505 sts [50 sts in each repeat]**

Rnd 14: sl2, (k2, k1 tbl, k1, k1 tbl, k5, k1 tbl, k3, k1 tbl, k5, sl2, k1, C3R{*sl2*}, k1, C3L{*sl2*}, sl2, k4, k1 tbl, k3, k1 tbl, k5, (k1 tbl, k1) twice) 10 times, k1, sl2.

Rnd 15: k2, (p2, C3R[*sl1, p1, sl1*], p5, sl1, p2, T2R{*sl1*}, p5, C5L, p1, pfbf, p1, C4L, p4, T2L{*sl1*}, p2, sl1, p5, C3L[*sl1, p1, sl1*], p1) 10 times, p1, k2. **525 sts [52 sts in each repeat]**

Rnd 16: sl2, (k2, k1 tbl, k1, k1 tbl, k5, k1 tbl,

k2, k1 tbl, k6, sl2, k1, sl2, k5, sl4, k5, k1 tbl, k2, k1 tbl, k5, (k1 tbl, k1) twice) 10 times, k1, sl2.

Rnd 17: k2, (p2, sl1, p1, T3L{*sl1*}, p3, sl1, T3R{*sl1*}, p4, T4R[*el.*], *p1*, T4L[*el.*], *p1*, T4R[*el.*], T4L[*el.*], p3, T3L{*sl1*}, sl1, p3, T3R{*sl1*}, p1, sl1, p1) 10 times, p1, k2.

Rnd 18: sl2, (k2, (k1 tbl, k3) twice, k2tbl, k6, sl2, k5, sl2, k1, sl2, k4, sl2, k5, k2tbl, (k3, k1 tbl) twice, k1) 10 times, k1, sl2.

Rnd 19: k2, (p2, sl1, p3, T3L{*sl1*}, p1, C2R{*sl2*}, p6, k2, p5, C5R, p4, T3L, p4, C2L{*sl2*}, p1, T3R{*sl1*}, p3, sl1, p1) 10 times, p1, k2.

Rnd 20: sl2, (k2, k1 tbl, k5, 3-into-1, k1 tbl, k6, sl2, k5, sl2, k1, sl2, k5, sl2, k4, k1 tbl, 3-into-1, k5, k1 tbl, k1) 10 times, k1, sl2.

485 sts [48 sts in each repeat]

Rnd 21: k2, (p2, (sl1, p6) twice, k2, p3, T4R[*el.*], *p1*, k2, p5, k2, p4, sl1, p6, sl1, p1) 10 times, p1, k2.

Rnd 22: sl2, (k2, (k1 tbl, k6) twice, sl2, k1, C4R{*sl2*}, k3, sl2, k5, sl2, k4, k1 tbl, k6, k1 tbl, k1) 10 times, k1, sl2.

Rnd 23: k2, (p2, (sl1, p6) twice, C5L, p4, T3R, p4, 1-into-5, k2, p4, sl1, p6, sl1, p1) 10 times, p1, k2. **525 sts [52 sts in each repeat]**

Rnd 24: sl2, (k2, (k1 tbl, k6) twice, sl2, k1, sl2, k4, sl2, k5, sl2, k1, sl4, k4, k1 tbl, k6, k1 tbl, k1) 10 times, k1, sl2.

Rnd 25: k2, (p2, T2L{*sl1*}, p4, T2R{*sl1*}, p4, T4R[*el.*], *p1*, T4L[*el.*], *p1*, T3R, p3, T4R[*el.*], *p1*, C4L, p4, T2L{*sl1*}, p4, T2R{*sl1*}, p1) 10 times, p1, k2.

Rnd 26: sl2, (k3, k1 tbl, k4, k1 tbl, (k5, sl2) twice, k1, sl2, k4, sl2, k3, sl4, k5, k1 tbl, k4, k1 tbl, k2) 10 times, k1, sl2.

Rnd 27: k2, (p3, T2L{*sl1*}, p2, T2R{*sl1*},

CHART C

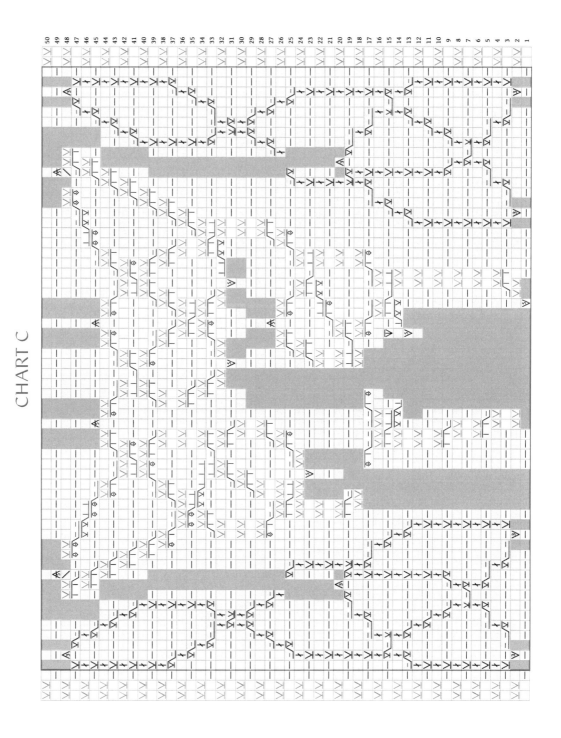

p4, T3R, p5, 5-into-1[*p*], p3, T3R, p3, k2, T4L[*el.*], p3, T2L{*sl1*}, p2, T2R{*sl1*}, p2) 10 times, p1, k2. **485 sts [48 sts in each repeat]**

Rnd 28: sl2, (k4, k1 tbl, k2, k1 tbl, k5, sl2, k10, sl2, k4, sl2, k2, sl2, k4, k1 tbl, k2, k1 tbl, k3) 10 times, k1, sl2.

Rnd 29: k2, (p4, T2L{*sl1*}, T2R{*sl1*}, p5, k2, p10, k2, p3, T3R, p2, k2, p4, T2L{*sl1*}, T2R{*sl1*}, p3) 10 times, p1, k2.

Rnd 30: sl2, (k5, k2tbl, k6, sl2, k10, (sl2, k3) twice, sl2, k5, k2tbl, k4) 10 times, k1, sl2.

Rnd 31: k2, (p5, C2R{*sl2*}, p6, k2, p2, (1-into-5, p3) twice, T3L, p1, T3R, p3, k2, p5, C2L{*sl2*}, p4) 10 times, p1, k2. **565 sts [56 sts in each repeat]**

Rnd 32: sl2, (k5, k2tbl, k6, sl2, C4R{*sl2*}, k1, sl2, k3, (sl2, k1, sl2, k4) twice, sl2, k5, k2tbl, k4) 10 times, k1, sl2.

Rnd 33: k2, (p3, T3R{*sl1*}, T2L{*sl1*}, p5, C4L, p3, T3L, T4R[*el.*], *p1*, T3L, p3, C5R, p3, T3R, p4, T2R{*sl1*}, T3L{*sl1*}, p2) 10 times, p1, k2.

Rnd 34: sl2, ((k3, k1 tbl) twice, k5, (sl4, k4) twice, sl2, k3, sl2, k1, C5L{*sl2*}, sl2, k5, k1 tbl, k3, k1 tbl, k2) 10 times, k1, sl2.

Rnd 35: k2, (p2, T2R{*sl1*}, p3, sl1, p4, T3R, k2, p4, C4L, p4, T3L, p2, k2, p4, C4L[*dbl. el.*], p5, sl1, p3, T2L{*sl1*}, p1) 10 times, p1, k2.

Rnd 36: sl2, (k2, (k1 tbl, k4) twice, sl2, k1, sl2, k4, sl4, k5, sl2, k2, sl2, k4, sl4, k5, k1 tbl, k4, k1 tbl, k1) 10 times, k1, sl2.

Rnd 37: k2, (p1, T2R{*sl1*}, p4, sl1, p3, T3R, p1, T3L, p2, T3R, T3L, p4, k2, p2, k2, p3, T3R, T4L[*el.*], p3, sl1, p4, T2L{*sl1*}) 10 times, p1, k2.

Rnd 38: sl2, (k1, k1 tbl, k5, k1 tbl, (k3, sl2) twice, (k2, sl2) twice, k4, sl2, k2, (sl2, k3) 3 times, k1 tbl, k5, k1 tbl) 10 times, k1, sl2.

Rnd 39: k2, (p1, sl1, p5, sl1, p2, T3R, p3, T3L, T3R, p2, T4L[*el.*], *p1*, T3R, p2, T3L, T4R[*el.*], p3, T3L, p2, sl1, p5, sl1) 10 times, p1, k2.

Rnd 40: sl2, (k1, k1 tbl, k5, k1 tbl, k2, sl2, k5, sl4, k5, sl2, k1, sl2, k4, sl4, k6, sl2, k2, k1 tbl, k5, k1 tbl) 10 times, k1, sl2.

Rnd 41: k2, (p1, sl1, p4, T2R{*sl1*}, p1, T3R, p5, C4R[*el.*], p5, C5R, p4, C4R[*el.*], p6, T3L, p1, T2L{*sl1*}, p4, sl1) 10 times, p1, k2.

Rnd 42: sl2, (k1, k1 tbl, k4, k1 tbl, k2, sl2, k6, sl4, k5, sl2, k1, sl2, k4, sl4, k7, sl2, k2, k1 tbl, k4, k1 tbl) 10 times, k1, sl2.

Rnd 43: k2, (p1, sl1, p3, T2R{*sl1*}, p1, T3R, p5, T3R, T4L[*el.*], *p1*, T4R[*el.*], *p1*, T4L[*el.*], *p1*, T3R, T4L[*el.*], p5, T3L, p1, T2L{*sl1*}, p3, sl1) 10 times, p1, k2.

Rnd 44: sl2, (k1, k1 tbl, k3, k1 tbl, k2, sl2, k6, sl2, k3, sl2, k1, sl2, k5, sl2, k1, sl2, k3, sl2, k6, sl2, k2, k1 tbl, k3, k1 tbl) 10 times, k1, sl2.

Rnd 45: k2, (p1, sl1, p2, T2R{*sl1*}, p1, T3R, p4, T4R[*dbl. el.*], p3, 5-into-1[*p*], p5, 5-into-1[*p*], p3, T4L[*dbl. el.*], p4, T3L, p1, T2L{*sl1*}, p2, sl1) 10 times, p1, k2. **485 sts [48 sts in each repeat]**

Rnd 46: sl2, (k1, (k1 tbl, k2) twice, sl2, k3, C4R{*sl2*}, k17, C4L{*sl2*}, k3, sl2, (k2, k1 tbl) twice) 10 times, k1, sl2.

Rnd 47: k2, (p1, sl1, p1, T2R{*sl1*}, p1, T3R, p1, T4R[*dbl. el.*], p21, T4L[*dbl. el.*], p1, T3L, p1, T2L{*sl1*}, p1, sl1) 10 times, p1, k2.

Rnd 48: sl2, (k1, 3-into-1, k2, sl2, k2tog, sl2, k25, sl2, ssk, sl2, k2, 3-into-1) 10 times, k1, sl2. **425 sts [42 sts in each repeat]**

Rnd 49: k2, (p4, 5-into-1[*p*], p25, 5-into-1[*p*], p3) 10 times, p1, k2. **345 sts [34 sts in each repeat]**

Rnd 50: sl2, k341, sl2.

DURROW

DURROW

The border for this modular triangular shawl is worked first, in a series of squares knitted in the round; the squares alternate between centre-out and centre-in, which allows the cable pattern to flow without interruption from one side of the border to the other.

After the border has been completed, stitches are picked up along the inside of the border, and the shawl body is worked upwards towards the neck using simple decreases, to create the triangular shape. The shawl is completed with an i-cord edging across the top edge, and a lace edging knitted on to the outer edge of the border.

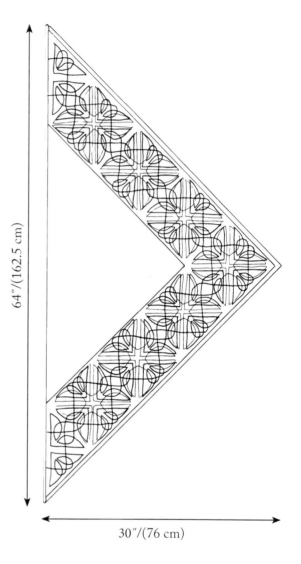

64″/(162.5 cm)

30″/(76 cm)

MATERIALS
- 3.0 mm/US size 2.5 DPNs (or needles for preferred method of working small circumferences in the round)
- One short (60 cm/24″ or shorter) 3.0 mm/ US size 2.5 circular needle (for border squares)
- One medium/long 3.0 mm/US size 2.5 circular needle (for shawl body)
- Cable needle
- **Malabrigo Sock Yarn** in the following shades:

    Aguas (Yarn A) - 2 skeins [620 yds/(567 m)]
    Abril (Yarn B) - 1 skein [190 yds/(174 m)]
    Zarzamora (Yarn C) - 1 skein [290 yds/(265 m)]
    Eggplant (Yarn D) -1 skein [355 yds/(325 m)]
- Waste yarn
- 1 stitch marker

GAUGE
23 sts and 39 rows over 4″/(10 cm), in stocking stitch after blocking

PATTERN NOTES

In this pattern, Yarn A is used for the main cable pattern that flows across the border, and Yarns B, C and D are used for the background cable pattern, which is self-contained within each square (see schematic and photographs). For the sample pictured, Yarn A is light turquoise, Yarn B is light purple, Yarn C is medium purple and Yarn D is dark purple. The gradual change in the colour of the background cable pattern creates a subtle variation in colour across the border, however this pattern would also work well with just one background colour (if using only one background colour, you will require approx. 835 yds/ (764 m), or 2 skeins, in total).

When working the cable pattern, Yarn A and the background yarn are striped on alternate rounds. Yarn A is used on all odd-numbered rounds, and the background yarn is used on all even-numbered rounds; when working with Yarn A, the stitches that form the contrasting background cable pattern are slipped whenever encountered (slip purlwise with yarn held at back of work), and vice versa when working with the background yarn. This creates the contrasting colour effect. Most of the cabling occurs on odd-numbered rounds.

Refer to the Chart Key & Abbreviations section (p. 73) for detailed information regarding elongated stitches.

CONSTRUCTION NOTES

The border for this shawl is worked first, as a series of squares (see general schematic on p. 38, and construction schematic on p. 40). First, squares are knitted from the centre-out, with the stitches of the final round left on waste yarn. Next, these stitches are picked up and connecting squares are worked inwards

to the centre (this attaches the squares to form the shape of the border). By alternating the sequence of centre-out and centre-in squares, the cable pattern is able to flow without interruption from one side of the border to the other. At each end of the border, 'corners' are worked; in order to be able to work with alternating colours on each row, it's necessary to work 1 RS row with Yarn A, 1 RS row with the background yarn, then 1 WS row with Yarn A, 1 WS row with the background yarn. This means that a small amount of WS cabling is required; in the Chart Key & Abbreviations section (p. 73), full directions are given for the cables which need to be worked on the WS.

Once the border is complete, stitches are picked up along the inner edge of the border, and the body of the shawl is worked towards the neck edge, shaped with simple decreases. Once the body is complete, an i-cord edging is worked along the top edge of the shawl, then a lace edging is worked around the outer edge of the border, with a small amount of short-row shaping at each corner and the centre point. Finally the end of the lace edging is grafted or sewn to the beginning of the i-cord edging.

DIRECTIONS

» Squares 1 & 2

With Yarn B, cast on 4 sts; join in Yarn
A at beginning of cast-on sts and p4.
Divide sts equally across 2 DPNs

Next rnd: with Yarn B, join to work in
the round, pm and k4.

Rnd 1: with Yarn A, work Rnd 1 of
Chart A (p. 44)/Chart A Written
Instructions (p. 43) 4 times.

Rnd 2: with Yarn B, work Rnd 2 of
Chart A 4 times.

Work from Chart A, using Yarn A on odd-
numbered rnds and Yarn B on even-numbered rnds,
distributing stitches over additional DPNs and then
short circular needle as st count increases.

Rnd 47: (work Rnd 47 of Chart A-II (p. 45)/
Chart A-II Written Instructions (p. 49) once,
work Rnd 47 of Chart A (p. 45)/Chart A Written
Instructions once) twice.

Continue to work from Chart A-II and Chart A
as set, until Rnd 51 of Chart A-II and Rnd 51 of
Chart A are complete.

Using four separate lengths of waste yarn, or four
separate stitch holders, and starting at beginning of
rnd, (sl 52 sts to waste yarn/stitch holder, sl 44 sts to
waste yarn/stitch holder) twice. Break yarn.

Work Square 2 identically to Square 1.

» Squares 3 & 4

Work Squares 3 & 4 identically to Squares 1 & 2,
using Yarn D instead of Yarn B.

» Square 5

With RS facing, sl 52 sts from waste yarn along
one Chart A-II edge of Square 1 to short circular

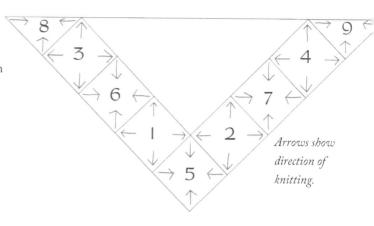

Arrows show direction of knitting.

needle; with waste yarn and Yarn A, provisionally
cast on 88 sts, breaking Yarn A at end of cast-on;
with RS still facing, sl 52 sts from waste yarn along
one Chart A-II edge of Square 2 to circular needle.

Set-up row: with RS facing, join in Yarn B; k1, ssk,
k16, sl2, k1, sl2, k5, sl2, k1, sl2, k16, k2tog; ((k1, ssk,
k39, k2tog) twice across provisionally cast on sts,
being careful not to twist cast-on), k1, ssk, k16, sl2,
k1, sl2, k5, sl2, k1, sl2, k16, k2tog. **184 sts**

Rnd 1: with Yarn A, work Rnd 1 of Chart B-II
(p. 46)/Chart B-II Written Instructions (p. 49),
(work Rnd 1 of Chart B (p. 46)/Chart B Written
Instructions (p. 49)) twice, work Rnd 1 of Chart B-II.

Rnd 2: Join in Yarn B and join to work in the round,
being careful not to twist, pm; work Rnd 2 of Chart
B-II, (work Rnd 2 of Chart B) twice, work Rnd 2 of
Chart B-II.

Continue to work from Chart B-II and Chart B as
set, using Yarn A on odd-numbered rnds and Yarn
B on even-numbered rnds, until Rnd 3 of Chart
B-II is complete. From Rnd 4 onwards, work each
rnd of Chart B 4 times across each rnd. After Rnd
50 is complete, p4 with Yarn A, then break yarn,

thread through remaining 4 sts and draw tight, pulling yarn ends to WS through centre of square; weave ends in on WS.

» Square 6

With RS facing, sl 52 sts from waste yarn along remaining Chart A-II edge of Square 1 to short circular needle; with waste yarn and Yarn A, provisionally cast on 44 sts, breaking Yarn A at end of cast-on; with RS still facing, sl 52 sts from waste yarn along one Chart A-II edge of Square 3 to circular needle; with waste yarn and Yarn A, provisionally cast on 44 sts.

Set-up row: with RS facing, join in Yarn C; k1, ssk, k16, sl2, k1, sl2, k5, sl2, k1, sl2, k16, k2tog; (k1, ssk, k39, k2tog) across provisionally cast on sts, being careful not to twist cast-on; k1, ssk, k16, sl2, k1, sl2, k5, sl2, k1, sl2, k16, k2tog; (k1, ssk, k39, k2tog) across provisionally cast on sts, being careful not to twist cast-on. **184 sts**

Rnd 1: with Yarn A, join to work in the round, being careful not to twist, pm; (work Rnd 1 of Chart B-II, work Rnd 1 of Chart B) twice.
Rnd 2: with Yarn C, (work Rnd 1 of Chart B-II, work Rnd 1 of Chart B) twice.

Continue as directed for Square 5.

» Square 7

Work Square 7 identically to Square 6 (using sts from edges of Squares 4 and 2).

» Corner 8

With RS facing, sl 52 sts from waste yarn along remaining Chart A-II edge of Square 3 to short circular needle; with waste yarn and Yarn A, provisionally cast on 44 sts, breaking Yarn A at end

of cast-on. **96 sts**
Set-up row: with WS facing, join in Yarn D; (p41, ssp, p1) across provisionally cast on sts; p2tog, p16, sl2 wyif, p1, sl2 wyif, p5, sl2 wyif, p1, sl2 wyif, p18, k1. **94 sts**
Row 1 [RS]: join in Yarn A, sl1, work Row 1 of Chart C-II (p. 48)/Chart C-II Written Instructions (p. 51), work Row 1 of Chart C (p. 48)/Chart C Written Instructions (p. 51), k1.
Row 2 [RS]: with RS still facing, slide sts back to right end of circular needle; with Yarn D, k1, work Row 2 of Chart C-II, work Row 2 of Chart C, sl1.
Row 3 [WS]: turn work to WS; with Yarn A, k1, work Row 3 of Chart C, work Row 3 of Chart C-II, sl1.
Row 4 [WS]: with WS still facing, slide sts back to right end of circular needle; with Yarn D, sl1, work Row 4 of Chart C twice, k1.

Continue to work from Chart C as set, alternating 2 RS rows and 2 WS rows, using Yarn A on odd-numbered rows and Yarn D on even-numbered rows. After Row 46 is complete, on WS with Yarn A, k1, k2tog twice, sl1; then break yarn, thread through remaining 4 sts and draw tight. Weave in ends.

» Corner 9

With waste yarn and Yarn A, provisionally cast on 44 sts to short circular needle, breaking Yarn A at end of cast-on; sl 52 sts from waste yarn along remaining Chart A-II edge of Square 4 to circular needle. **96 sts**
Set-up row: with WS facing, join in Yarn D; p18, sl2 wyif, p1, sl2 wyif, p5, sl2 wyif, p1, sl2 wyif, p16, ssp, p1; (p2tog, p42) across provisionally cast on sts. **94 sts**
Row 1 [RS]: join in Yarn A, sl1, work Row 1 of Chart C, work Row 1 of Chart C-II, k1.
Row 2 [RS]: with RS still facing, slide sts back to right end of circular needle; with Yarn D, k1, work Row 2 of Chart C, work Row 2 of Chart C-II, sl1.

Row 3 [WS]: turn work to WS; with Yarn A, k1, work Row 3 of Chart C-II, work Row 3 of Chart C, sl1.
Row 4 [WS]: with WS still facing, slide sts back to right end of circular needle; with Yarn D, sl1, work Row 4 of Chart C twice, k1.

Continue as directed for Corner 8.

BODY

With RS facing, and beginning at inner edge of border, using long circ needle, sl 44 sts from waste yarn at edge of Square 4, sl 44 sts from waste yarn at cast-on edge of Square 7, sl 44 sts from waste yarn at edge of Square 2, sl 44 sts from waste yarn at edge of Square 1, sl 44 sts from waste yarn at cast-on edge of Square 6, sl 44 sts from waste yarn at edge of Square 3. **264 sts** on circ needle.

Row 1 [RS]: join in Yarn D, k2, k2tog, k128, pm, M1, k to last 4 sts, ssk, k2. 263 sts
Row 2: [WS]: sl1 wyif, p to last st, k1.
Row 3: with Yarn C, sl1, k1, k2tog, k to 2 sts before m, ssk, sl m, k1, k2tog, k to last 4 sts, ssk, k2. **259 sts**
Row 4: as Row 2.

With Yarn D, work Rows 3 - 4. Continue to repeat Rows 3 - 4, alternating Yarns C and D, until 11 sts remain.
Next row [RS]: sl1, k1, k2sl1psso, remove marker, k1, k2sl1psso, k2. **7 sts**
Next row [WS]: sl1, p1, p2sl1psso, p1, k1. **5 sts**
Next row [RS]: k1, k2sl1psso, k1. **3 sts**

Break yarn, draw through rem sts and pull tight. Weave ends in securely.

I-CORD EDGING

With long circular needle and Yarn A, with RS facing, pick up and k 46 sts along top edge of Corner 9, pick up and k 180 sts along slipped sts at top edge of triangle, pick up and k 46 sts along top edge of Corner 8, break yarn. **272 sts** on circular needle.

With Yarn A, cast on 4 sts to a DPN. Work i-cord for 5 rows as follows: k4, slide sts to other end of needle, work next row with a second DPN without turning work.
Next row: with RS facing, sl 4 sts of i-cord to circular needle holding picked up and knitted sts (at beginning of row). k3, ssk with one st from circular needle.
Next row: sl 4 sts just worked back to circular needle; k3, ssk with one st from circular needle.

Continue to work i-cord across top edge until all sts from circular needle have been used up. Work a further 4 rows in unattached i-cord, then work set up row to begin lace edging as follows, after slipping sts back to ln: (k2tog, sl st back to ln) 3 times; without turning work pick up and k 4 sts along edge of rows just worked. **5 sts** on DPN.

Sl all sts on waste yarn along lower edge of border to long circular needle; with a removable stitch marker or safety pin, mark the point inbetween sts at the bottom corner of Square 5. **440 sts** on circular needle.

Returning to i-cord sts still on DPN, k 1 st from circular needle, then turn and p 6 sts.

LACE EDGING

Short Row 1 [RS]: sl1, k1, w&t.
Short Row 2[WS]: p1, k1.
Short Row 3: sl1, ssk, yo, k1, k2tog, w&t.
Short Row 4: p2tog, yo, k1, p1, k1
See p. 43 for Lace Edging Chart.
Lace Edging Row 1: sl1, ssk, yo, k2, p2tog with one st from circular needle.
Lace Edging Row 2: sl1 wyif, p2tog, yo, k1, p1, k1.

Lace Edging Rows 3-4: as Rows 1-2.

Lace Edging Row 5: sl1, ssk, yo, k2, p3tog with 2 sts from circular needle.

Lace Edging Row 6: as Row 2.

Work Lace Edging until the last st before removable stitch marker/safety pin is worked with lace edging, finishing on a WS row.

Short Row 1 [RS]: sl1, ssk, yo, k2, w&t.

Short Row 2 [WS]: p2tog, yo, k1, p1, k1.

Short Row 3: sl1, ssk, yo, k1, w&t.

Short Row 4: sl1, yo, k1, p1, k1.

Short Row 5: sl1, w&t.

Short Row 6: k1.

From this point onwards, when working into sts that have been wrapped, pick up wrap and work with stitch.

Short Row 7: sl1, k1, w&t.

Short Row 8: p1, k1.

Short Row 9: sl1, ssk, yo, k1, k2tog, w&t.

Short Row 10: p2tog, yo, k1, p1, k1.

Continue to work Lace Edging as previously set, until

1 st remains on circular needle, finishing on a WS row.

Short Row 1 [RS]: sl1. ssk, yo, k1, w&t.

Short Row 2 [WS]: sl1, yo, k1, p1, k1.

Short Row 3: sl1, w&t.

Short Row 4: k1.

Final row: sl1, ssk, yo, k1, k2tog twice.

FINISHING

Break yarn and either cast-off all sts and sew to edge of i-cord, or graft live sts to edge of i-cord. Weave in all ends, using ends to close up any holes at corners of squares, and block shawl to finished measurements.

LACE EDGING CHART

CHART WRITTEN INSTRUCTIONS

Please note that the stitch counts at the end of each round (or row) refer only to the stitches in each repeat (refer to Directions beginning on p. 40 for number of repeats for each square or corner).

CHART A WRITTEN INSTRUCTIONS

Rnd 1: pfb. **2 sts**

Rnd 2: k1, 1-into-5. **6 sts**

Rnd 3: p1, M1p, sl2, p1, sl2, M1p. **8 sts**

Rnd 4: k all sts.

Rnd 5: p1, M1p, T3R{*sl2*}, p1, T3L{*sl2*}, M1p. **10 sts**

Rnd 6: k all sts.

Rnd 7: p1, M1p, T3R{*sl2*}, p1, 1-into-5, p1, T3L{*sl2*}, M1p. **16 sts**

Rnd 8: 1-into-7, k5, sl2, k1, sl2, k5. *At end of this rnd remove marker, sl 3 sts from ln to rn, replace marker.* **22 sts**

Rnd 9: p2, sl2, T3R{*sl2*}, p2, k2, p1, k2, p2, T3L{*sl2*}, sl2, p1.

Rnd 10: k2, k2[*el.*], k5, sl2, k1, sl2, k5, k2[*el.*], k1.

Rnd 11: p2, C4L{*sl4*}, M1p, p2, T3R, p1,

CHART A

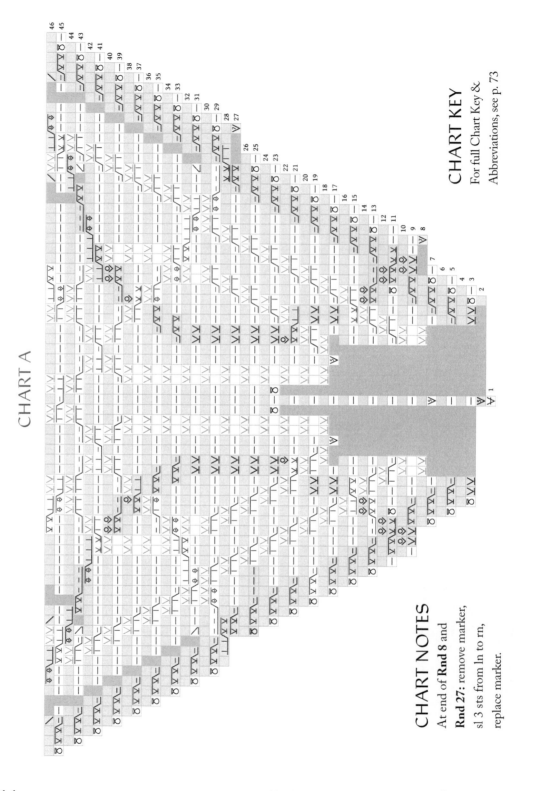

CHART KEY

For full Chart Key &
Abbreviations, see p. 73

CHART NOTES

At end of **Rnd 8** and
Rnd 27: remove marker,
sl 3 sts from ln to rn,
replace marker.

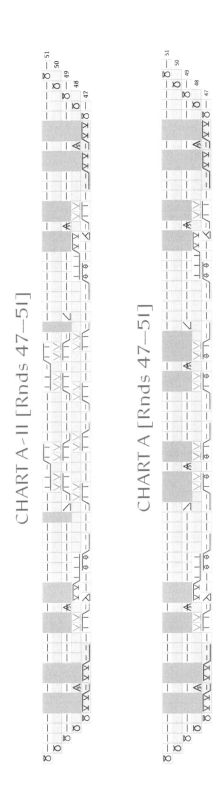

CHART A-II [Rnds 47–51]

CHART A [Rnds 47–51]

T3L, p2, M1p, C4L{*sl4*}, p1. **24 sts**

Rnd 12: k4, k2[*el.*], (k3, sl2) twice, k3, k2[*el.*], k3.

Rnd 13: p1, M1p, T3R{*sl2*}, T4L{*sl2*}, T3R, p3, T3L, T4R{*sl2*}, T3L{*sl2*}, M1p. **26 sts**

Rnd 14: k7, k2[*el.*], sl2, k5, sl2, k2[*el.*], k6.

Rnd 15: p1, M1p, T3R{*sl2*}, p3, C4R{*k2*} [sl2], p5, C4R{*sl2*}, p3, T3L{*sl2*}, M1p. **28 sts**

Rnd 16: k8, sl2, k9, sl2, k7.

Rnd 17: p1, M1p, T3R{*sl2*}, p3, T3R, sl2, (p1, 1-into-5) twice, p1, sl2, T3L, p3, T3L{*sl2*}, M1p. **38 sts**

Rnd 18: k8, sl2, k4, (sl2, k1) 3 times, sl2, k4, sl2, k7.

Rnd 19: p1, M1p, T3R{*sl2*}, p3, T3R, p1, sl2, T3R, (p1, k2) twice, p1, T3L, sl2, p1, T3L, p3, T3L{*sl2*}, M1p. **40 sts**

Rnd 20: k8, sl2, k4, sl2, k2, sl2, k1, sl2, k2, sl2, k4, sl2, k7.

Rnd 21: p1, M1p, T3R{*sl2*}, p3, T3R, p2, C4L{*sl2*}, p2, k2, p1, k2, p2, C4L[*sl2*]{*k2*}, p2, T3L, p3, T3L{*sl2*}, M1p. **42 sts**

Rnd 22: k8, sl2, k3, sl2, k1, k1[*el.*], k2, sl2, k1, sl2, k2, k1[*el.*], k1, sl2, k3, sl2, k7.

Rnd 23: p1, M1p, T3R{*sl2*}, p3, T3R, p2, T3R, sl2, p2, k2, M1p, p1, M1p, k2, p2, sl2, T3L, p2, T3L, p3, T3L{*sl2*}, M1p. **46 sts**

Rnd 24: k8, (sl2, k3, sl2, k5) twice, sl2, k3, sl2, k7.

Rnd 25: p1, M1p, T3R{*sl2*}, p3, T3R, p2, T3R, p1, sl2, p2, k2, p3, k2, p2, sl2, p1, T3L, p2, T3L, p3, T3L{*sl2*}, M1p. **48 sts**

Rnd 26: k8, (sl2, k3, sl2, k6) twice, sl2, k3, sl2, k7.

Rnd 27: 1-into-7, T3R{*sl2*}, p3, (T3R, p2) twice, sl2, p2, k2, p3, k2, p2, sl2, (p2, T3L) twice, p3, T3L{*sl2*}. *At end of this rnd remove marker, sl 3 sts from ln to rn, replace marker.* **54 sts**

Rnd 28: k2, C4R{*k2*}[*sl2*], k4, (sl2, k3, sl2,

DURROW

k7) twice, sl2, k3, sl2, k4, C4R{*sl2*}, k1.

Rnd 29: p1, M1p, T3R{*sl2*}, T5L[*dbl. el.*], T3R, p2, T3R, p3, sl2, p2, k2, p3, k2, p2, sl2, p3, T3L, p2, T3L, T5R[*dbl. el.*], T3L{*sl2*}, M1p. **56 sts**

Rnd 30: k8, sl4, (k3, sl2, k8, sl2) twice, k3, sl4, k7.

Rnd 31: p1, M1p, T3R{*sl2*}, p2tog, p2, C4L[*dbl. el.*], p3, k2, p4, sl2, p2, k2, p3, k2, p2, sl2, p4, k2, p3, C4L[*dbl. el.*]{*k2*}, p2, ssp, T3L{*sl2*}, M1p.

Rnd 32: k8, sl2, C5L{*sl2*}, sl2, k8, sl2, k3, sl2, k8, sl2, C5R{*sl2*}, sl2, k7.

Rnd 33: p1, M1p, T3R{*sl2*}, p3, T3R, p3, C4R{*k2*}[*dbl. el.*], p3, T3R{*sl2*}, p2, k2, p3, k2, p2, T3L{*sl2*}, p3, C4R[*dbl. el.*], p3, T3L, p3, T3L{*sl2*}, M1p. **58 sts**

Rnd 34: k8, sl2, k4, sl4, k8, sl2, k3, sl2, k8, sl4, k4, sl2, k7.

Rnd 35: p1, M1p, T3R{*sl2*}, p3, T3R, p4, k2, T4L[*el.*], T3R{*sl2*}, (p3, k2) twice, p3, T3L{*sl2*}, T4R[*el.*], k2, p4, T3L, p3, T3L{*sl2*}, M1p. **60 sts**

Rnd 36: k8, sl2, k5, sl2, k2, sl2, k6, sl2, k3, sl2, k6, sl2, k2, sl2, k5, sl2, k7.

Rnd 37: p1, M1p, T3R{*sl2*}, p3, T3R, p5, k2, p2, C4L[*sl2*]{*k2*}, p4, k2, p3, k2, p4, C4L{*sl2*}, p2, k2, p5, T3L, p3, T3L{*sl2*}, M1p. **62 sts**

Rnd 38: k8, sl2, k6, sl2, k3, k1[*el.*], sl2, k4, sl2, k3, sl2, k4, sl2, k1[*el.*], k3, sl2, k6, sl2, k7.

Rnd 39: p1, M1p, T3R{*sl2*}, p3, T3R, p6, k2, T4R{*sl2*}, T4L, p1, T3R, p3, T3L, p1, T4R, T4L{*sl2*}, k2, p6, T3L, p3, T3L{*sl2*}, M1p. **64 sts**

Rnd 40: k8, sl2, k7, sl2, k2[*el.*], k4, sl2, k1, sl2, k5, sl2, k1, sl2, k4, k2[*el.*], (sl2, k7) twice.

Rnd 41: p1, M1p, T3R{*sl2*}, p3, T3R, p7, C4R{*sl2*}, p4, C5R, p5, C5R, p4, C4R{*k2*}

CHART B [Rnds 1–3]

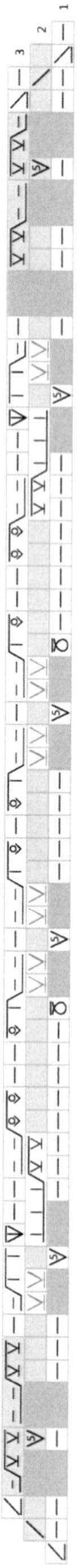

CHART B-II [Rnds 1–3]

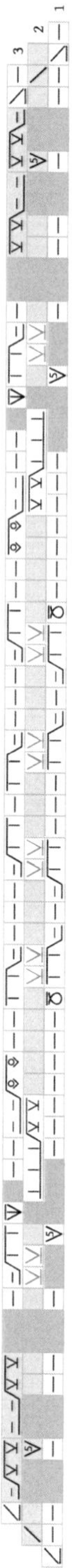

CHART B

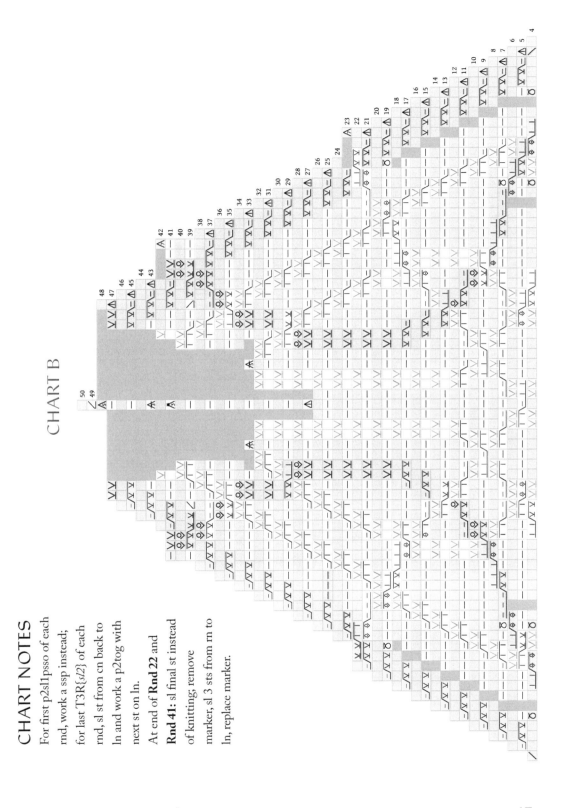

CHART NOTES

For first p2sl1psso of each rnd, work a ssp instead; for last T3R{*sl2*} of each rnd, sl st from cn back to ln and work a p2tog with next st on ln.

At end of **Rnd 22** and **Rnd 41**: sl final st instead of knitting; remove marker, sl 3 sts from rn to ln, replace marker.

CHART NOTES

At beginning of **Row 21**, work k3tog in place of 5-into-1[*p*]; at end of Row 21, work k3tog using final 3 sts.

CHART C

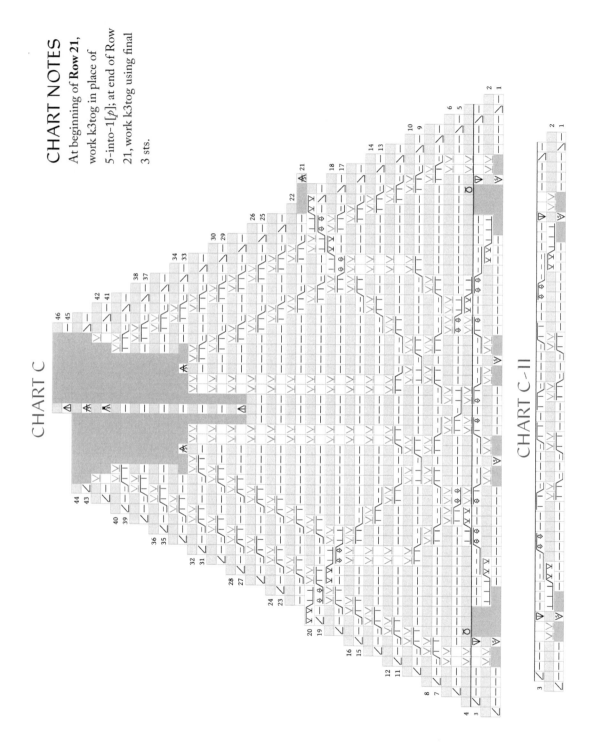

CHART C-II

[sl2], p7, T3L, p3, T3L{*sl2*}, M1p. **66 sts**

Rnd 42: k8, sl2, k5, C5R[*dbl. el.*], sl2, k4, sl2, k1, sl2, k5, sl2, k1, sl2, k4, sl2, C5L[*dbl. el.*], k5, sl2, k7.

Rnd 43: p1, M1p, T3R{*sl2*}, p3, T3R, p2tog, T5R{*sl2*}, p3, T4L, T4R, p1, T4L, p1, T4R, p1, T4L, T4R, p3, T5L{*sl2*}, ssp, T3L, p3, T3L{*sl2*}, M1p.

Rnd 44: k8, sl2, C4R[*dbl. el.*], k8, sl4, k5, sl2, k1, sl2, k5, sl4, k8, C4L[*dbl. el.*], sl2, k7.

Rnd 45: p1, M1p, T3R{*sl2*}, p4, C4L[*sl2*]{*k2*}, p10, C4L[*dbl. el.*]{*k2*}, p5, C5L, p5, C4L[*dbl. el.*], p10, C4L{*sl2*}, p4, T3L{*sl2*}, M1p. **68 sts**

Rnd 46: k4, k2tog, k1, C4R[*dbl. el.*], sl2, k2tog, k6, C4R{*sl2*}, sl2, k5, sl2, k1, sl2, k5, sl2, C4L{*sl2*}, k6, ssk, sl2, C4L[*dbl. el.*], k1, ssk, k3. **64 sts**

Rnd 47: p1, M1p, T3R{*sl2*}, T4R{*sl2*}, p1, T3R, p3 tog, p2, T4R[*dbl. el.*], p2, T4L[*el.*], *p1*, T4R[*el.*], *p1*, T4L[*el.*], *p1*, T4R[*el.*], p2, T4L[*dbl. el.*], p2, sssp, T3L, p1, T4L{*sl2*}, T3L{*sl2*}, M1p. **62 sts**

Rnd 48: k1, M1, k1, 5-into-1, k3, sl2, k1, C5R{*sl2*}, k6, sl2, k1, sl2, k5, sl2, k1, sl2, k6, C5L{*sl2*}, k1, sl2, k3, 5-into-1, k1, M1. **56 sts**

Rnd 49: p1, M1p, p6, 5-into-1[*p*], p7, p2tog, 5-into-1[*p*], p5, 5-into-1[*p*], ssp, p7, 5-into-1[*p*], p6, M1p. **40 sts**

Rnd 50: k1, M1, k39, M1. **42 sts**

Rnd 51: p1, M1p, p41, M1p. **44 sts**

CHART A-II WRITTEN INSTRUCTIONS

Rnd 47: p1, M1p, T3R{*sl2*}, T4R{*sl2*}, p1, T3R, p3 tog, p2, T4R[*dbl. el.*], p2, T3L, p3, T3R, p1, T3L, p3, T3R, p2, T4L[*dbl. el.*], p2,

sssp, T3L, p1, T4L{*sl2*}, T3L{*sl2*}, M1p. **62 sts**

Rnd 48: k1, M1, k1, 5-into-1, k3, sl2, k1, C5R{*sl2*}, k5, (sl2, k3) 3 times, sl2, k5, C5L{*sl2*}, k1, sl2, k3, 5-into-1, k1, M1. **56 sts**

Rnd 49: p1, M1p, p6, 5-into-1[*p*], p6, p2tog, T3L, p1, T3R, p3, T3L, p1, T3R, ssp, p6, 5-into-1[*p*], p6, M1p. **48 sts**

Rnd 50: k1, M1, k16, sl2, k1, sl2, k5, sl2, k1, sl2, k16, M1. **50 sts**

Rnd 51: p1, M1p, p17, C5R, p5, C5R, p17, M1p. **52 sts**

CHART B-II WRITTEN INSTRUCTIONS

Rnd 1: p1, ssp, p6, 1-into-5, p7, M1p, T3R, p1, T3L, p3, T3R, p1, T3L, M1p, p7, 1-into-5, p6, p2tog. **58 sts**

Rnd 2: k1, ssk, k1, 1-into-5, k3, sl2, k1, C5L{*sl2*}, k5, (sl2, k3) 3 times, sl2, k5, C5R{*sl2*}, k1, sl2, k3, 1-into-5, k1, k2tog. **64 sts**

Rnd 3: p1, ssp, T3L{*sl2*}, T4L{*sl2*}, p1, T3L, pfbf, p2, T4L[*dbl. el.*], p2, T3R, p3, T3L, p1, T3R, p3, T3L, p2, T4R[*dbl. el.*], p2, pfbf, T3R, p1, T4R{*sl2*}, T3R{*sl2*}, p2tog. **66 sts**

CHART B WRITTEN INSTRUCTIONS

Rnd 1: p1, ssp, p6, 1-into-5, p8, M1p, 1-into-5, p5, 1-into-5, M1p, p8, 1-into-5, p6, p2tog. **58 sts**

Rnd 2: k1, ssk, k1, 1-into-5, k3, sl2, k1, C5L{*sl2*}, k6, sl2, k1, sl2, k5, sl2, k1, sl2, k6, C5R{*sl2*}, k1, sl2, k3, 1-into-5, k1, k2tog. **64 sts**

Rnd 3: p1, ssp, T3L{*sl2*}, T4L{*sl2*}, p1, T3L, pfbf, p2, T4L[*dbl. el.*], p2, T4R[*el.*], *p1*, T4L[*el.*], *p1*, T4R[*el.*], *p1*, T4L[*el.*], p2, T4R[*dbl. el.*], p2, pfbf, T3R, p1, T4R{*sl2*},

T3R{*sl2*}, p2tog. **66 sts**

Rnd 4: k1, ssk, k3, M1, k1, C4L[*dbl. el.*], sl2, M1, k7, C4L{*sl2*}, sl2, k5, sl2, k1, sl2, k5, sl2, C4R[*sl2, k2*], k7, M1, sl2, C4R[*dbl. el.*], k1, M1, k3, k2tog. **68 sts**

For first p2sl1psso of each foll rnd, work a ssp instead; for last T3R{sl2} of each rnd (except Rnds 21 and 41): sl st from cn back to ln and work a p2tog with next st on ln.

Rnd 5: p2sl1psso, T3L{*sl2*}, p4, C4L{*sl2*}, p10, C4L[*dbl. el.*], p5, C5L, p5, C4L[*dbl. el.*]{*k2*}, p10, C4L[*sl2, k2*], p4, T3R{*sl2*}. **66 sts**

Rnd 6: k8, sl2, C4L[*dbl. el.*], k8, sl4, k5, sl2, k1, sl2, k5, sl4, k8, C4R[*dbl. el.*], sl2, k7.

Rnd 7: p2sl1psso, T3L{*sl2*}, p3, T3L, p1, M1p, T5L{*sl2*}, p3, T4R, T4L, p1, T4R, p1, T4L, p1, T4R, T4L, p3, T5R{*sl2*}, M1p, p1, T3R, p3, T3R{*sl2*}.

Rnd 8: k8, sl2, k5, C5L[*dbl. el.*], sl2, k4, sl2, k1, sl2, k5, sl2, k1, sl2, k4, sl2, C5R[*dbl. el.*], k5, sl2, k7.

Rnd 9: p2sl1psso, T3L{*sl2*}, p3, T3L, p7, C4R[*k2, sl2*], p4, C5R, p5, C5R, p4, C4R[*sl2, k2*], p7, T3R, p3, T3R{*sl2*}. **64 sts**

Rnd 10: k8, sl2, k7, sl2, k2[*el.*], k4, sl2, k1, sl2, k5, sl2, k1, sl2, k4, k2[*el.*], (sl2, k7) twice.

Rnd 11: p2sl1psso, T3L{*sl2*}, p3, T3L, p6, k2, T4L{*sl2*}, T4R, p1, T3L, p3, T3R, p1, T4L, T4R{*sl2*}, k2, p6, T3R, p3, T3R{*sl2*}. **62 sts**

Rnd 12: k8, sl2, k6, sl2, k3, k1[*el.*], sl2, k4, sl2, k3, sl2, k4, sl2, k1[*el.*], k3, sl2, k6, sl2, k7.

Rnd 13: p2sl1psso, T3L{*sl2*}, p3, T3L, p5, k2, p2, C4L{*sl2*}, p4, k2, p3, k2, p4, C4L[*sl2, k2*], p2, k2, p5, T3R, p3, T3R{*sl2*}. **60 sts**

Rnd 14: k8, sl2, k5, sl2, k2, sl2, k6, sl2, k3, sl2, k6, sl2, k2, sl2, k5, sl2, k7.

Rnd 15: p2sl1psso, T3L{*sl2*}, p3, T3L,

p4, k2, T4R[*el.*], T3L{*sl2*}, (p3, k2) twice, p3, T3R{*sl2*}, T4L[*el.*], k2, p4, T3R, p3, T3R{*sl2*}. **58 sts**

Rnd 16: k8, sl2, k4, sl4, k8, sl2, k3, sl2, k8, sl4, k4, sl2, k7.

Rnd 17: p2sl1psso, T3L{*sl2*}, p3, T3L, p3, C4R[*dbl. el.*], p3, T3L{*sl2*}, p2, k2, p3, k2, p2, T3R{*sl2*}, p3, C4R{*k2*}[*dbl. el.*], p3, T3R, p3, T3R{*sl2*}. **56 sts**

Rnd 18: k8, sl2, C5R{*sl2*}, sl2, k8, sl2, k3, sl2, k8, sl2, C5L{*sl2*}, sl2, k7.

Rnd 19: p2sl1psso, T3L{*sl2*}, M1p, p3, C4L[*dbl. el.*]{*k2*}, p3, k2, p4, sl2, p2, k2, p3, k2, p2, sl2, p4, k2, p3, C4L[*dbl. el.*], p3, M1p, T3R{*sl2*}.

Rnd 20: k8, sl4, (k3, sl2, k8, sl2) twice, k3, sl4, k7.

Rnd 21: p2sl1psso, T3L{*sl2*}, T5R[*dbl. el.*], T3L, p2, T3L, p3, sl2, p2, k2, p3, k2, p2, sl2, p3, T3R, p2, T3R, T5L[*dbl. el.*], T3R{*sl2*}. **54 sts**

Rnd 22: k2, C4R[*sl2, k2*], k4, (sl2, k3, sl2, k7) twice, sl2, k3, sl2, k4, C4R[*k2, sl2*], k1.

At end of this rnd, sl final st instead of knitting; remove marker, sl 3 sts from rn to ln, replace marker.

Rnd 23: 7-into-1, T3L{*sl2*}, p3, (T3L, p2) twice, sl2, p2, k2, p3, k2, p2, sl2, (p2, T3R) twice, p3, T3R{*sl2*}. **48 sts**

Rnd 24: k8, (sl2, k3, sl2, k6) twice, sl2, k3, sl2, k7.

Rnd 25: p2sl1psso, T3L{*sl2*}, p3, T3L, p2, T3L, p1, sl2, p2, k2, p3, k2, p2, sl2, p1, T3R, p2, T3R, p3, T3R{*sl2*}. **46 sts**

Rnd 26: k8, (sl2, k3, sl2, k5) twice, sl2, k3, sl2, k7.

Rnd 27: p2sl1psso, T3L{*sl2*}, p3, T3L, p2, T3L, sl2, p2, k2, p2sl1psso, k2, p2, sl2, T3R, p2, T3R, p3, T3R{*sl2*}. **42 sts**

Rnd 28: k8, sl2, k3, sl2, k2[*el.*], k2, sl2, k1, sl2, k2, k2[*el.*], sl2, k3, sl2, k7.

Rnd 29: p2sl1psso, T3L{*sl2*}, p3, T3L, p2, C4L[*sl2, k2*], p2, k2, p1, k2, p2, C4L{*sl2*}, p2, T3R, p3, T3R{*sl2*}. **40 sts**

Rnd 30: k8, sl2, k4, sl2, k2, sl2, k1, sl2, k2, sl2, k4, sl2, k7.

Rnd 31: p2sl1psso, T3L{*sl2*}, p3, T3L, p1, sl2, T3L, (p1, k2) twice, p1, T3R, sl2, p1, T3R, p3, T3R{*sl2*}. **38 sts**

Rnd 32: k8, sl2, k4, (sl2, k1) 3 times, sl2, k4, sl2, k7.

Rnd 33: p2sl1psso, T3L{*sl2*}, p3, T3L, sl2, (p1, 5-into-1[*p*]) twice, p1, sl2, T3R, p3, T3R{*sl2*}. **28 sts**

Rnd 34: k8, sl2, k2[*el.*], k5, k2[*el.*], sl2, k7.

Rnd 35: p2sl1psso, T3L{*sl2*}, p3, C4R[*sl2, k2*], p5, C4R[*k2, sl2*], p3, T3R{*sl2*}. **26 sts**

Rnd 36: k7, k2[*el.*], sl2, k5, sl2, k2[*el.*], k6.

Rnd 37: p2sl1psso, T3L{*sl2*}, T4R{*sl2*}, T3L, p3, T3R, T4L{*sl2*}, T3R{*sl2*}. **24 sts**

Rnd 38: k4, k2[*el.*], (k3, sl2) twice, k3, k2[*el.*], k3.

Rnd 39: p2, C4L{*sl4*}, ssp, p1, T3L, p1, T3R, p1, p2tog, C4L{*sl4*}, p1. **22 sts**

Rnd 40: k2, k2[*el.*], k5, sl2, k1, sl2, k5, k2[*el.*], k1.

Rnd 41: p2, sl2, T3L{*sl2*}, p2, k1, 3-into-1[*sl*], k1, p2, T3R{*sl2*}, sl2, p1. **20 sts** *At end of this rnd, sl final st instead of knitting; remove marker, sl 3 sts from rn to ln, replace marker.*

Rnd 42: 7-into-1, k5, sl1, k1, sl1, k5. **14 sts**

Rnd 43: p2sl1psso, T3L{*sl2*}, p1, 3-into-1[*p*], p1, T3R{*sl2*}. **10 sts**

Rnd 44: k all sts.

Rnd 45: p2sl1psso, T3L{*sl2*}, p1, T3R{*sl2*}. **8 sts**

Rnd 46: k all sts.

Rnd 47: p2sl1psso, sl2, p1, sl2. **6 sts**

Rnd 48: k1, 5-into-1. **2 sts**

Rnd 49: p2tog. 1 st

Rnd 50: k all sts.

CHART C-II WRITTEN INSTRUCTIONS

Row 1: p1, ssp, p4, 1-into-5, p9, T3R, p1, T3L, p3, T3R, p1, T3L, p9, 1-into-5, p4, p2tog. **56 sts**

Row 2: k6, sl2, k1, C5L{*sl2*}, k6, (sl2, k3) 3 times, sl2, k6, C5R{*sl2*}, k1, sl2, k5.

Row 3: k2tog, k3, p2, kfb, k3, T5R[*dbl. el.*], k2, T3L, k3, T3R, k1, T3L, k3, T3R, k2, T5L[*dbl. el.*], k3, kfb, p2, k3, ssk, k1.

CHART C WRITTEN INSTRUCTIONS

Row 1: p1, ssp, p4, 1-into-5, p10, 1-into-5, p5, 1-into-5, p10, 1-into-5, p4, p2tog. **56 sts**

Row 2: k6, sl2, k1, C5L{*sl2*}, k7, sl2, k1, sl2, k5, sl2, k1, sl2, k7, C5R{*sl2*}, k1, sl2, k5.

Row 3: k2tog, k3, p2, kfb, k3, T5R[*dbl. el.*], k2, T4L[*el.*], k1, T4R[*el.*], k1, T4L[*el.*], k1, T4R[*el.*], k2, T5L[*dbl. el.*], k3, kfb, p2, k3, ssk, k1.

Row 4: p4, sl2 p1, M1p, p8, C4R{*sl2*}, sl2 p5, sl2 p1, sl2 p5, sl2 C4L{*sl2*}, p8, M1p, p1, sl2 p5. **60 sts**

Row 5: p1, ssp, p2, k2, p12, C4L[*dbl. el.*], p5, C5L, p5, C4L[*dbl. el.*]{*k2*}, p12, k2, p2, p2tog. **58 sts**

Row 6: k4, sl2, k12, sl4, k5, sl2, k1, sl2, k5, sl4, k12, sl2, k3.

Row 7: k2tog, k1, T3R, k9, T4L, T4R, k1, T4L, k1, T4R, k1, T4L, T4R, k9, T3L, k1, ssk, k1. **56 sts**

Row 8: p3, sl2 p9, sl2 p4, sl2 p1, sl2 p5, sl2 p1, sl2 p4, sl2 p9, sl2 p4.

Row 9: p1, ssp, p1, T3L, p6, T4R, p4, C5R, p5, C5R, p4, T4L, p6, T3R, p1, p2tog. **54 sts**

Row 10: k4, (sl2, k6) 2 times, sl2, k1, sl2, k5, sl2, k1, (sl2, k6) 2 times, sl2, k3.

Row 11: k2tog, k1, T3R, k5, p2, k4, T4L, k1, T3R, k3, T3L, k1, T4R, k4, p2, k5, T3L, k1, ssk, k1. **52 sts**

Row 12: p3, sl2 p5, (sl2 p4) 2 times, sl2 p3, (sl2 p4) 2 times, sl2 p5, sl2 p4.

Row 13: p1, ssp, p1, T3L, p4, k2, p2, T4R, p4, k2, p3, k2, p4, T4L, p2, k2, p4, T3R, p1, p2tog. **50 sts**

Row 14: (k4, sl2) 2 times, k2, sl2, k6, sl2, k3, sl2, k6, sl2, k2, sl2, k4, sl2, k3.

Row 15: k2tog, k1, T3R, k3, p2, T4L, k6, p2, k3, p2, k6, T4R, p2, k3, T3L, k1, ssk, k1. **48 sts**

Row 16: p3, sl2 p3, sl4, p8, sl2 p3, sl2 p8, sl4, p3, sl2 p4.

Row 17: p1, ssp, p1, T3L, p2, C4L[*dbl. el.*] {*k2*}, p8, k2, p3, k2, p8, C4L[*dbl. el.*], p2, T3R, p1, p2tog. **46 sts**

Row 18: k4, sl2, C4R{*sl2*}, sl2, k8, sl2, k3, sl2, k8, sl2, C4L{*sl2*}, sl2, k3.

Row 19: k2tog, k1, C4R{*k2*} [*dbl. el.*], k2, T3R, k7, p2, k3, p2, k7, T3L, k2, C4R[*dbl. el.*], k1, ssk, k1. **44 sts**

Row 20: C4L{*sl2*}, (sl2 p3, sl2 p7) 2 times, sl2 p3, sl2 C4R{*sl2*}, p1.

Row 21: *At beginning of this row work k3tog in place of 5–into–1[p]; at end of this row work k3tog using final 3 sts.* 5-into-1[*p*], (p2, T3L) 2 times, p6, k2, p3, k2, p6, (T3R, p2) 2 times. **40 sts**

Row 22: k4, (sl2, k3, sl2, k6) 2 times, (sl2, k3) 2 times.

Row 23: k2tog, k1, T3R, k2, T3R, k5, p2, k3, p2, k5, T3L, k2, T3L, k1, ssk, k1. **38 sts**

Row 24: p3, (sl2 p3, sl2 p5) 2 times, sl2 p3, sl2 p4.

Row 25: p1, ssp, p1, T3L, p2, T3L, p4, k2, p3, k2, p4, T3R, p2, T3R, p1, p2tog. **36 sts**

Row 26: (k4, sl2, k3, sl2) 3 times, k3.

Row 27: k2tog, k1, T3R, k2, T3R, k3, p2, sl1k2psso, p2, k3, T3L, k2, T3L, k1, ssk, k1. **32 sts**

Row 28: (p3, sl2) 3 times, p1, (sl2 p3) 2 times, sl2 p4.

Row 29: p1, ssp, p1, (T3L, p2) 2 times, k2, p1, k2, (p2, T3R) 2 times, p1, p2tog. **30 sts**

Row 30: k4, sl2, k3, sl2, k2, sl2, k1, sl2, k2, (sl2, k3) 2 times.

Row 31: k2tog, k1, T3R, k2, T3R, (k1, p2) 2 times, k1, T3L, k2, T3L, k1, ssk, k1. **28 sts**

Row 32: p3, sl2 p3, (sl2 p1) 3 times, sl2 p3, sl2 p4.

Row 33: p1, ssp, p1, T3L, p2, 5-into-1[*p*], p1, 5-into-1[*p*], p2, T3R, p1, p2tog. **18 sts**

Row 34: k4, sl2, k7, sl2, k3.

Row 35: k2tog, k1, T3R, k5, T3L, k1, ssk, k1. **16 sts**

Row 36: p3, sl2 p5, sl2 p4.

Row 37: p1, ssp, p1, T3L, p3, T3R, p1, p2tog. **14 sts**

Row 38: k4, (sl2, k3) 2 times.

Row 39: k2tog, k1, T3R, k1, T3L, k1, ssk, k1. **12 sts**

Row 40: p3, sl2 p1, sl2 p4.

Row 41: p1, ssp, p1, k1, 3-into-1[sl], k1, p1, p2tog. **8 sts**

Row 42: k3, sl1, k1, sl1, k2.

Row 43: k2tog, 3-into-1[*p*], ssk, k1. **4 sts**

Row 44: p all sts.

Row 45: p1, p2sl1psso. **2 sts**

Row 46: k all sts.

KELLS

KELLS

Kells is a seamless pullover worked from the top down and entirely in the round.

The Celtic knot motif is repeated four times across the pullover (on the front, back and down each sleeve); slipped stitch cables provide a contrasting colour effect.

SIZES

Sizes: 1 (2, 3, 4, 5){6, 7, 8, 9}(10, 11, 12)

*For detailed information on choosing a size and finished measurements, refer to **Sizing & Fit** section on p. 57.*

MATERIALS

• 3.75 mm/US size 5 needles (**or size needed to obtain gauge**)
• 3.5 mm/US size 4 needles (or one size below gauge-size needles, for ribbing):
For each size, you will need:
• 1 short circ needle for yoke/collar
• 1 medium/long circ needle for body/hem
• DPNs (or needles for preferred method of working small circumferences in the round) for sleeves/cuffs
• Cable needle
• 13 stitch markers (1 unique for beginning-of-rnd; 8 for marking charts; 4 for marking sleeves)
• **Malabrigo Arroyo** - see p. 59 for information on yarn shades and quantities
If substituting a different yarn, choose a DK/light-worsted weight yarn that knits to the specified gauge

GAUGE

18.5 sts and 29 rnds over 4″/(10 cm), in stocking stitch after blocking

Matching gauge is imperative to the finished measurements; the needle sizes listed are only a suggestion and should be changed if necessary. Measure gauge in the rnd, after wet-blocking swatch and leaving to dry completely

SIZING & FIT

Select your size by referring to the Sizing Chart on p. 58. The Sizing Chart shows the finished measurements of the pullover. Select the size closest to your body measurements (for a close fit, as pictured), or select a size with finished measurements approx. 2—3″/(5–7.5 cm) larger (for a more relaxed fit).

If you're unsure which size to select, try measuring a pullover in a similar weight yarn which fits you well, and compare these measurements to the Sizing Chart to find your size. The sample shown is Size 1 on a 5′ 2″/(157.5 cm) tall model with 34″/(86.5 cm) bust.

This pullover features some shaping at the bust, waist and hips; if you prefer, you can omit the shaping and simply knit straight down after the yoke separation (note that you will need a multiple of 4 stitches for the k2, p2 rib at the hem, so it may be necessary to inc/dec a few stitches).

The placement of the cable motif is on the centre back, centre front and the centre of each sleeve; this means that the spacing between the motifs is larger in the larger sizes, and that the cable motif will look proportionately smaller. This is illustrated in the two roughly-to-scale schematics below, which show Size 1 and Size 9.

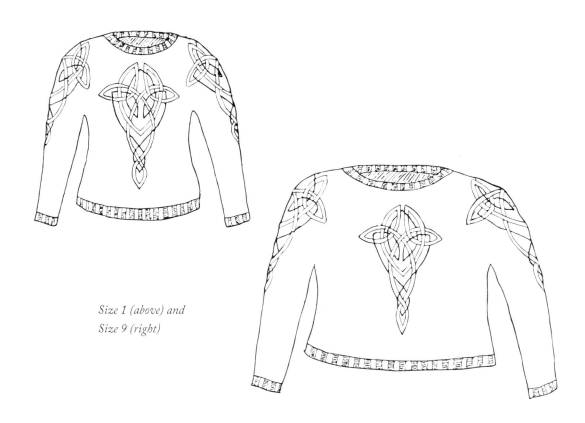

*Size 1 (above) and
Size 9 (right)*

SIZING CHART

	1	2	3	4	5	6	7	8	9	10	11	12	
COLLAR CIRCUMFERENCE													
	20 ¾	**20 ¾**	21 ½	**23 ¼**	24 ¼	**24 ¼**	25	**26 ¾**	27 ¾	**27 ¾**	28 ½	**28 ½**	″
	52	*52*	*54*	*58.5*	*60.5*	*60.5*	*62.5*	*67*	*69*	*69*	*71.5*	*71.5*	*cm*
BODY CIRCUMFERENCE AT UNDERARM													
	33 ½	**35 ½**	36 ¼	**38 ½**	40 ¼	**42**	45 ¼	**47**	49	**50 ¾**	52	**53 ¼**	″
	84	*89*	*90.5*	*96.5*	*100.5*	*105*	*113.5*	*117.5*	*122*	*126.5*	*130*	*133.5*	*cm*
BUST (approx. 2″/(5 cm) below underarm)													
	34 ½	**36 ¾**	39	**41 ¼**	43	**45**	47 ¼	**49**	51 ¼	**53 ½**	56	**57 ¾**	″
	86.5	*92*	*97.5*	*103*	*107*	*112.5*	*118.5*	*122.5*	*128*	*134*	*140*	*144*	*cm*
WAIST													
	27 ¾	**29 ½**	32	**34 ¼**	36	**37 ½**	40 ¼	**42**	44 ½	**46 ¼**	48 ½	**49 ¾**	″
	69	*73.5*	*80*	*85.5*	*89.5*	*94*	*100.5*	*105*	*111.5*	*115.5*	*121*	*124.5*	*cm*
HIP													
	32	**33 ¾**	36 ¼	**39**	40 ¾	**42 ½**	45	**46 ¾**	49 ¼	**51**	52 ¾	**54 ½**	″
	80	*84.5*	*91*	*97.5*	*101.5*	*106*	*112.5*	*117*	*123*	*127.5*	*132*	*136*	*cm*
UPPER ARM CIRCUMFERENCE													
	11 ¾	**12 ¼**	12 ¼	**13 ¼**	14	**14 ½**	15 ¾	**15 ¾**	16 ¼	**17 ¼**	18 ¼	**18 ½**	″
	29	*30.5*	*30.5*	*33*	*35*	*36*	*39.5*	*39.5*	*40.5*	*43*	*45.5*	*46*	*cm*
FRONT YOKE DEPTH													
	8	**8 ¼**	8 ½	**8 ¾**	8 ¾	**8 ¾**	9 ½	**9 ½**	9 ¾	**10**	10 ¼	**10 ¼**	″
	16.5	*17*	*18*	*18.5*	*18.5*	*18.5*	*20*	*20*	*20.5*	*21.5*	*22*	*22*	*cm*
BACK YOKE DEPTH													
	10	**10 ¼**	10 ½	**10 ¾**	10 ¾	**10 ¾**	11 ¼	**11 ¼**	11 ½	**11 ¾**	12 ¼	**12 ¼**	″
	25	*25.5*	*26*	*27*	*27*	*27*	*28.5*	*28.5*	*29*	*29.5*	*30.5*	*30.5*	*cm*
UNDERARM TO HEM													
	12 ¼	**11 ¾**	11 ¾	**11 ¾**	11 ¾	**11 ½**	11 ½	**11 ¼**	11 ¼	**11 ¼**	11 ¼	**11 ¼**	″
	30.5	*29.5*	*29.5*	*29.5*	*29.5*	*29*	*29*	*28.5*	*28.5*	*28.5*	*28.5*	*28.5*	*cm*
SLEEVE UNDERARM TO WRIST													
	16 ¾	**17**	17 ¾	**17 ¾**	18	**18**	18	**18**	18	**18**	18 ¼	**18 ¼**	″
	42	*43*	*44*	*44*	*45*	*45*	*45*	*45*	*45*	*45*	*45.5*	*45.5*	*cm*
WRIST CIRCUMFERENCE													
	7 ¾	**7 ¾**	7 ¾	**7 ¾**	7 ¾	**8 ¾**	8 ¾	**8 ¾**	8 ¾	**9 ½**	9 ½	**9 ½**	″
	19.5	*19.5*	*19.5*	*19.5*	*19.5*	*21.5*	*21.5*	*21.5*	*21.5*	*24*	*24*	*24*	*cm*

YARN REQUIREMENTS

Size	1	2	3	4	5	6	7	8	9	10	11	12	
Yarn A	560	580	615	645	670	705	740	755	790	835	865	880	yds
	512	530	562	590	613	645	677	690	722	764	791	805	m
Yarn B	480	495	525	555	575	605	635	645	680	720	745	755	yds
	439	453	480	507	526	553	581	590	622	658	681	690	m
Yarn C	110	110	120	125	130	135	140	145	150	160	160	165	yds
	101	101	110	114	119	123	128	133	137	146	146	151	m

Malabrigo Arroyo, skeins required [(335 yds/306 m per 100g)]

	1	2	3	4	5	6	7	8	9	10	11	12	
Reflecting Pool (A)	2	2	2	2	2	3	3	3	3	3	3	3	skeins
Regatta Blue (B)	2	2	2	2	2	2	2	2	3	3	3	3	skeins
Glitter (C)	1	1	1	1	1	1	1	1	1	1	1	1	skein

PATTERN NOTES

In this pattern, Yarn A is used for the main (thicker) strand of the cable pattern, and Yarn B is used for the thinner twisted-stitch strand. Yarn A and Yarn B are striped on alternate rounds. Yarn A is used on all odd-numbered rounds, and Yarn B is used on all even-numbered rounds; when working with Yarn A, the stitches that form the contrasting Yarn B cable pattern are slipped whenever encountered (always slip purlwise with yarn held at back of work), and vice versa when working with Yarn B. This creates the contrasting colour effect. Most of the cabling occurs on odd-numbered rounds. See the section Combining Colours (p. 9) for more information on how to choose and swatch colour combinations.

When changing from Yarn A to Yarn B (and vice versa) at the beginning of each round, be careful to maintain an even tension (if your tension here is too tight or too loose, it may form a visible ladder at the back left edge of the yoke; if the change in tension is only slight, this should disappear after washing and blocking).

Refer to the Chart Key & Abbreviations section (p. 73) for detailed information regarding elongated stitches.

When working the short-row shaping at the back of the neck, Yarn A and Yarn B need to be changed on each row, to maintain the single-stripe pattern. To achieve this, you can either use a yarn-joining method such as a spit-splice or Russian join, or break the yarn, join in the new yarn and then weave in all of the ends after the short-row shaping is complete (if breaking the yarn, a good way to maintain even tension at the k2 before the w&t

is to k1 holding both colours together, break old yarn, continue working with new yarn; when next encountering the stitch with both colours worked together, work normally as 1 stitch).

It's important to use a stretchy cast-on at the collar, and a stretchy cast-off at the cuffs and hem. A suggested cast-off to use over the k2, p2 rib is: k2, sl 2 sts back to ln, ssk, *(p1, sl 2 sts back to ln, p2tog) twice, (k1, sl 2 sts back to ln, ssk) twice; rep from * until all sts are cast off. If you wish the cast-on edge to exactly match the cast-off edges, begin the collar with a provisional cast-on and use a matching cast-off after the cuffs and hem have been completed.

CONSTRUCTION NOTES

This pullover is worked from the top-down, entirely in the round and without any seams. The cable motif is repeated 4 times across the yoke, and increases are worked in the spaces between the motifs. When directed to inc evenly, space out the incs randomly and try to avoid making them at the same point where incs have been made on the previous rnd (this creates a circular-type yoke, without any raglan lines). After the yoke has been completed, the sleeve sts are slipped onto a holder/waste yarn, sts are cast on at the underarm and then the body is worked down towards the hem, with bust, waist and hip shaping. After the body is complete, sts are picked up at the underarm cast-on, then each sleeve is worked down towards the cuff.

DIRECTIONS
YOKE
Collar to Shoulder

Using Yarn C and a stretchy cast-on, cast on 96 (96, 100, 108, 112){112, 116, 124, 128}(128, 132, 132) sts to short circ smaller needles, pm and join to work in the round. Work in k2, p2 rib for 11 rnds.

Next rnd: switch to short circ gauge-size needles, k all sts, inc 16 sts evenly across rnd. **112 (112, 116, 124, 128){128, 132, 140, 144}(144, 148, 148) sts**

Break Yarn C, join in Yarn A.

Short Row 1 [RS]: k36 (36, 38, 42, 44){44, 46, 50, 52}(52, 54, 54), break Yarn A, join in Yarn B, w&t.
Short Row 2 [WS]: p16 (16, 18, 22, 24){24, 26, 30, 32}(32, 34, 34), break Yarn B, join in Yarn A, w&t.

Short Row 3 [RS]: k to previous turning point, picking up and working wrap with st, k2, break Yarn A, join in Yarn B, w&t.
Short Row 4 [WS]: p to previous turning point, picking up and working wrap with st, p2, break Yarn B, join in Yarn A, w&t.

Repeat instructions for Short Rows 3 and 4 a further 5 times (7 short row pairs in total).

Next rnd [RS]: with Yarn A, k all sts to end of rnd, picking up and working remaining wrap.
Next rnd: with Yarn B, k all sts.
Rep last 2 rnds once more.

Next rnd [inc rnd]: With Yarn A, k all sts, inc 16 sts evenly across rnd. **128 (128, 132, 140, 144){144, 148, 156, 160}(160, 164, 164) sts**

Continuing to alternate Yarn A and Yarn B on each rnd, work a further 1 (1, 1, 1, 1){5, 3, 3, 3}(3, 3, 3) rnds even, work inc rnd a further 0 (0, 0, 0, 0){0, 0, 0, 0}(1, 1, 1) times, then work 0 (0, 0, 0, 0){0, 2, 2, 2}(1, 1, 1) rnd(s) even. **128 (128, 132, 140, 144){144, 148, 156, 160}(176, 180, 180) sts**

Break both Yarn A and Yarn B, remove beginning of rnd marker, sl 16 (16, 17, 18, 18){18, 19, 20, 20} (22, 23, 23) sts from ln to rn, replace marker for new beginning of rnd.

Rnd 1: Join in Yarn A, k5 (5, 5, 6, 7){7, 7, 8, 9}(11, 11, 11), pm, work Cable Chart Rnd 1 (p. 67)/ Written Instructions Rnd 1 (p. 66), pm, [k9 (9, 10, 12, 13){13, 14, 16, 17}(21, 22, 22), pm, work Cable Chart Rnd 1, pm], 3 times, k4 (4, 5, 6, 6){6, 7, 8, 8}(10, 11, 11). **160 (160, 164, 172, 176){176, 180, 188, 192}(208, 212, 212) sts,** 9 (9, 10, 12, 13){13, 14, 16, 17}(21, 22, 22) sts in each plain section.

From this point onwards, the cable chart sections will be contained within markers (these will be shifted at certain points); the plain sections between the cable chart sections will contain increases on some rnds. Note that the beginning-of-rnd marker is positioned in the centre of the first plain section (this corresponds to the back left of the pullover). St counts are given for the plain sections whenever they change (note that when the chart markers are shifted, the plain section st counts will also change). Switch to longer circ needles when necessary.

Rnd 2: join in Yarn B, [k to m, work Cable Chart Rnd 2 to next m] 4 times, k to end.

Rnd 3 (and all subsequent rnds): continue to work as set from the cable chart, using Yarn A on odd-numbered rnds and Yarn B on even-numbered rnds.

Rnd 5: inc 3 sts before first chart repeat, [work Cable Chart Rnd 5, inc 6 sts in plain section] 3 times, work Cable Chart Rnd 5, inc 3 sts in final plain section. 24 sts increased. **192 (192, 196, 204, 208){208, 212, 220, 224}(240, 244, 244) sts,** 15 (15, 16, 18, 19){19, 20, 22, 23}(27, 28, 28) sts in each plain section.

Continue up to and including Rnd 10.

Rnd 11: inc 2 sts before first chart repeat, [work Cable Chart Rnd 11, inc 4 sts in plain section] 3 times, work Cable Chart Rnd 11, inc 2 sts in final plain section. 16 sts increased. **216 (216, 220, 228, 232){232, 236, 244, 248}(264, 268, 268) sts,** 19 (19, 20, 22, 23){23, 24, 26, 27}(31, 32, 32) in each plain section.

Continue as set to Rnd 14. On Rnd 15, remove chart markers as they are encountered, whilst working incs as follows:

Rnd 15: inc 2 sts before first chart repeat, [work Cable Chart Rnd 15, inc 4 sts in plain section] 3 times, work Cable Chart Rnd 15, inc 2 sts in final plain section. 16 sts increased. **232 (232, 236, 244, 248){248, 252, 260, 264}(280, 284, 284) sts,** 23 (23, 24, 26, 27){27, 28, 30, 31}(35, 36, 36) sts in each plain section.

Rnd 16: replace chart markers as follows: k3 (3, 3, 4, 5){5, 5, 6, 7}(9, 9, 9), [pm, k9, work Cable Chart Rnd 16, k9, pm, k5 (5, 6, 8, 9){9, 10, 12, 13}(17, 18, 18)] 3 times, pm, k2 (2, 3, 4, 4){4, 5, 6, 6}(8, 9, 9).

Yoke Increases

Rnd 17 [Yoke inc rnd]: inc 1 st before first chart repeat, [work Cable Chart Rnd 17 (p. 69)/Written Instructions Rnd 17 (p. 66), inc 2 sts in plain section] 3 times, work Cable Chart, inc 1 st in final plain section. **8 sts increased. 272 (272, 276, 284, 288){288, 292, 300, 304}(320, 324, 324) sts,** 7 (7, 8, 10, 11){11, 12, 14, 15}(19, 20, 20) sts in each plain section.

Continue as set, working 2 further yoke inc rnds on **Rnd 19** and **Rnd 21** (on Rnd 21, remove chart markers as they are encountered).

After Rnd 21, st count is 304 **(304, 308, 316, 320){320, 324, 332, 336}(352, 356, 356) sts**, 11 (11, 12, 14, 15){15, 16, 18, 19}(23, 24, 24) sts in each plain section.

Rnd 22: replace chart markers as follows: k1 (1, 1, 2, 3){3, 3, 4, 5}(7, 7, 7), [pm, k5, work Cable Chart Rnd 22, k5, pm, k1 (1, 2, 4, 5){5, 6, 8, 9}(13, 14, 14)] 3 times, pm, k0 (0, 1, 2, 2){2, 3, 4, 4}(6, 7, 7).

Work yoke inc rnd on **Rnd 23**; 312 **(312, 316, 324, 328){328, 332, 340, 344}(360, 364, 364) sts**, 3 (3, 4, 6, 7){7, 8, 10, 11}(15, 16, 16) sts in each plain section.

Work yoke inc rnd every 6 rnds a further 1 (2, 2, 2, 2){2, 2, 2, 2}(2, 2, 2) times; 5 (7, 8, 10, 11){11, 12, 14, 15}(19, 20, 20) sts in each plain section.

Continue as set to Rnd 40. On Rnd 40, remove chart markers as they are encountered.

Rnd 41: replace chart markers as follows: k11 (12, 12, 13, 14){14, 14, 15, 16}(18, 18, 18), [pm, work Cable Chart Rnd 41 (p. 70)/Written Instructions Rnd 41 (p. 68), pm, k21 (23, 24, 26, 27){27, 28, 30, 31}(35, 36, 36)] 3 times, pm, k10 (11, 12, 13, 13){13, 14, 15, 15}(17, 18, 18). 288 **(296, 300, 308, 312){312, 316, 324, 328}(344, 348, 348) sts**, 21 (23, 24, 26, 27){27, 28, 30, 31}(35, 36, 36) sts in each plain section.

» Sizes 6-12 only
Continue as set, working a yoke inc rnd on **Rnd 43**, then every 6 rnds a further - (-, -, -, -){0, 1, 1, 2}(2, 2, 3) times. - **(-, -, -, -){320, 332, 340, 328}(344, 348, 348) sts,** - (-, -, -, -){29, 32, 34, 37}(41, 42, 44) sts in each plain section.

» All sizes
Continue as set up to and including Rnd 51 (53, 53,

53, 53){51, 55, 55, 57}(59, 61, 61).

Next rnd [Rnd 52 (54, 54, 54, 54){52, 56, 56, 58}(60, 62, 62)]: Position 4 new markers for sleeve separation as follows: k to first chart repeat, work Cable Chart, k16 (18, 19, 21, 21){23, 24, 26, 28}(30, 30, 31), pm for sleeve, k5 (5, 5, 5, 6){6, 8, 8, 9}(11, 12, 13), work Cable Chart, k4 (5, 5, 5, 5){6, 8, 8, 9}(11, 12, 12), pm for sleeve, k17 (18, 19, 21, 22){23, 24, 26, 28}(30, 30, 32), work Cable Chart, k16 (18, 19, 21, 21){23, 24, 26, 28}(30, 30, 31), pm for sleeve, k5 (5, 5, 5, 6){6, 8, 8, 9}(11, 12, 13), work Cable Chart, k4 (5, 5, 5, 5){6, 8, 8, 9}(11, 12, 12), pm for sleeve, k6 (6, 7, 8, 8){8, 8, 9, 9}(9, 9, 10) to end of rnd.

Next rnd [underarm inc rnd]: work across rnd as set, working an M1 increase 1 st before and 1 st after each sleeve marker. 8 sts increased. 280 **(280, 284, 292, 296){312, 308, 316, 328}(344, 332, 340) sts,** 23 (25, 26, 28, 29){31, 34, 36, 39}(43, 44, 46) sts in each plain section.

Continue as set working a underarm inc rnd every 2 rnds a further 1 (1, 2, 3, 3){4, 3, 3, 2}(1, 0, 0) times, finishing on Rnd 56 (58, 60, 62, 62){62, 64, 64, 64}(64, 64, 64); (if finishing on Rnd 64, remove chart markers as they are encountered). 280 **(280, 292, 292, 296){312, 316, 324, 328}(336, 332, 340) sts,** 25 (27, 30, 34, 35){39, 40, 42, 43}(45, 44, 46) sts in each plain section.

» Sizes 1-6 only
Continue to Sleeve Separation section.

» Sizes 7-12 only
Rnd 65: work underarm inc rnd **whilst at the same time** replacing chart markers as follows: k - (-, -, -, -){-, 25, 26, 28}(30, 30, 31), pm, work Cable Chart Rnd 65 (p. 71)/Written Instructions Rnd 65 (p. 70), pm, k to 1 st before sleeve m, M1, k1, sl

sleeve m, k1, M1, k - (-, -, -, -){-, 20, 20, 20}(21, 21, 22), pm, work Cable Chart Rnd 65, pm, k to 1 st before sleeve m, M1, k1, sl sleeve m, k1, M1, k - (-, -, -, -){-, 36, 38, 39}(40, 39, 41), pm, work Cable Chart Rnd 65, pm, k to 1 st before sleeve m, M1, k1, sl sleeve m, k1, M1, k- (-, -, -, -){-, 20, 20, 20}(21, 21, 22), pm work Cable Chart Rnd 65, pm, k to 1 st before sleeve m, M1, k1, sl sleeve m, k1, M1, k - (-, -, -, -){-, 11, 12, 11}(10, 9, 10) to end of rnd. - (-, -, -, -){-, 324, 332, 336}(344, 340, 348) sts, - (-, -, -, -){-, 60, 62, 63}(65, 64, 66) sts in each plain section.

Continue as set, working underarm inc rnd every 2 rnds a further - (-, -, -, -){-, 0, 0, 1}(2, 3, 3) times, finishing on Rnd - (-, -, -, -){-, 66, 66, 68}(70, 72, 72). - (-, -, -, -){-, 324, 332, 344}(360, 364, 372) sts, - (-, -, -, -){-, 60, 62, 65}(69, 70, 72) sts in each plain section.

Sleeve Separation

» *All sizes*

Next rnd [Rnd 57 (59, 61, 63, 63){63, 67, 67, 69}(71, 73, 73)]: break Yarn A and Yarn B leaving enough length to weave in later, remove beginning-of-rnd marker, sl 8 (8, 10, 12, 12){13, 13, 14, 14}(14, 14, 15) sts from rn to ln, remove sleeve marker.

With Yarn A and medium length circ needles, [cast on 4 (4, 4, 4, 5){5, 6, 6, 6}(6, 7, 7) sts, without breaking yarn work across back of pullover as set to sleeve marker, remove marker and sl 58 (57, 59, 57, 58){61, 65, 65, 67}(71, 73, 74) sleeve sts to holder/waste yarn, remove next sleeve marker, cast on 4 (5, 5, 4, 6){5, 6, 6, 6}(6, 8, 8) sts, pm for side-seam, cast on 4 (4, 4, 4, 5){5, 6, 6, 6}(6, 7, 7) sts, work across front of pullover as set to sleeve marker, remove marker and sl 58 (57, 59, 57, 58){61, 65, 65, 67}(71, 73, 74) sleeve sts to holder/waste yarn, remove next sleeve marker, cast on 4 (5, 5,

4, 6){5, 6, 6, 6}(6, 8, 8) sts.

Next rnd: join in Yarn B and work across rnd as set (note that due to breaking yarn, work will not technically be joined in the rnd until next rnd); for Sizes 4, 5 and 6 remove chart markers on this rnd. **176 (184, 184, 194, 202){210, 218, 226, 234}(242, 248, 254) sts** for body, 88 (92, 96, 97, 101){105, 109, 113, 117}(121, 124, 127) sts on each side for front and back, 58 (57, 59, 57, 58){61, 65, 65, 67}(71, 73, 74) sts held for each sleeve. 43 (43, 39, 39, 39){39, 21, 21, 21}(21, 21, 21) sts between chart markers on front and back.

BODY

» *All sizes*

Body Rnd 1: pm for beginning of rnd, join in Yarn A, and work across round as set.

Continue as set for a further 7 rnds.

» *Sizes 1-6 only*

When you reach Rnd 65, which will be on Body Rnd 7 (5, 3, 1, 1) {1, -, -, -} (-, -, -), replace chart markers as follows: k32 (34, 36, 38, 40){42, -, -, -}(-, -, -), pm, work Cable Chart Rnd 65 (p. 71)/Written Instructions Rnd 65 (p. 70), pm, k to side-seam marker, k32 (34, 36, 38, 40){42, -, -, -}(-, -, -), pm, work Cable Chart Rnd 65, pm, k to end of rnd.

» *All sizes*

Next rnd [Body Rnd 9]: work across back, working Cable Chart Rnd 67 (69, 71, 73, 73){73, 77, 77, 79}(81, 83, 83), k to side-seam marker, k to chart marker inc'g 0 (1, 2, 2, 2){3, 4, 4, 5}(6, 8, 9) sts evenly, work Cable Chart Rnd 67 (69, 71, 73, 73){73, 77, 77, 79}(81, 83, 83), k to end of rnd inc'g 0 (1, 2, 2, 2){3, 4, 4, 5}(6, 8, 9) sts evenly. **168 (178, 188, 198, 206){216, 226, 234, 244}(254, 264, 272) sts;** 84 (88, 92, 97, 101){105, 109, 113, 117}(121,

124, 127) sts on back, 84 (90, 96, 101, 105){111, 117, 121, 127}(133, 140, 145) sts on front. 21 sts between chart markers.

Work 7 (7, 5, 5, 5){5, 5, 5, 7}(7, 9, 7) rnds even.

Waist shaping

Note that during the following waist shaping rounds the end of the Cable Chart will be reached; after completing Cable Chart Rnd 106, k the remaining 15 sts for the remainder of the body (chart markers can either be removed at this point or left in place to help with counting stitches).

Next rnd [Body Rnd 17 (17, 15, 15, 15){15, 15, 15, 17}(17, 19, 17)]: k5 (5, 5, 5, 6){6, 6, 6, 7}(7, 7, 7), k2tog, k across back working Cable Chart Rnd 75 (77, 77, 79, 79){79, 83, 83, 87}(89, 93, 91), k to 7 (7, 7, 7, 8){8, 8, 8, 9}(9, 9, 9) sts before side-seam marker, ssk, k5 (5, 5, 5, 6){6, 6, 6, 7}(7, 7, 7), sl m, k5 (5, 5, 5, 6){6, 6, 6, 7}(7, 7, 7), k2tog, k to chart marker dec'g 0 (1, 2, 2, 2){3, 4, 4, 3}(3, 4, 5) sts evenly, work Cable Chart Rnd 75 (77, 77, 79, 79){79, 83, 83, 87}(89, 93, 91), k to 7 (7, 7, 7, 8){8, 8, 8, 9}(9, 9, 9) sts before beginning-of-rnd marker whilst at the same time dec'g 0 (1, 2, 2, 2){3, 4, 4, 3}(3, 4, 5) sts evenly, ssk, k5 (5, 5, 5, 6){6, 6, 6, 7}(7, 7, 7) to end of rnd.
164 (172, 180, 190, 198){206, 214, 222, 234}(244, 252, 258) sts; 82 (86, 90, 95, 99){103, 107, 111, 115} (119, 122, 125) sts on back, 82 (86, 90, 95, 99){103, 107, 111, 119}(125, 130, 133) sts on front. 21 sts between chart markers.

Work 5 (3, 5, 5, 5){5, 5, 5, 7}(7, 7, 9) rnds even.

» Sizes 9-12 only

Next rnd [Body Rnd - (-, -, -, -){-, -, -, 25}(25, 27, 27)]: k7, k2tog, k to 9 sts before side-seam marker, ssk, k7, sl m, k7, k2tog, k to chart marker dec'g - (-, -, -, -){-, -, -, 2}(3, 4, 4) sts evenly, k to 9 sts before beginning-of-rnd marker whilst at the same time dec'g - (-, -, -, -){-, -, -, 2}(3, 4, 4) sts evenly, ssk, k7 to end of rnd. - **(-, -, -, -){-, -, -, 226}(234, 236, 242) sts;** - (-, -, -, -){-, -, -, 113}(117, 118, 121) sts on both front and back. - (-, -, -, -){-, -, -, 21}(21, 19, 19) sts between chart markers.

Work - (-, -, -, -){-, -, -, 7}(7, 7, 9) rnds even.

» All sizes

Next rnd [waist shaping dec rnd]: k5 (5, 5, 5, 6) {6, 6, 6, 7}(7, 7, 7), k2tog, k across back working Cable Chart as set, k to 7 (7, 7, 7, 8){8, 8, 8, 9}(9, 9, 9) sts before side-seam marker, ssk, k5 (5, 5, 5, 6){6, 6, 6, 7}(7, 7, 7), sl m, k5 (5, 5, 5, 6){6, 6, 6, 7} (7, 7, 7), k2tog, k across front working Cable Chart as set, k to 7 (7, 7, 7, 8){8, 8, 8, 9}(9, 9, 9) sts before beginning-of-rnd marker, ssk, k5 (5, 5, 5, 6){6, 6, 6, 7}(7, 7, 7) to end of rnd.
160 (168, 176, 186, 194){202, 210, 218, 218}(226, 224, 230) sts; 80 (84, 88, 93, 97){101, 105, 109, 109}(113, 112, 115) sts on both front and back. 21 (21, 21, 21, 21) {21, 21, 21, 19}(19, 15, 15) sts between chart markers.

Continue as set, working a waist shaping dec rnd every 6 (4, 6, 6, 6){6, 6, 6, 0}(0, 0, 0) rnds a further 2 (5, 3, 3, 3){2, 3, 3, 0}(0, 0, 0) times, then every 4 (0, 4, 4, 4){4, 0, 0, 6}(6, 0, 0) rnds a further 3 (0, 1, 1, 1){2, 0, 0, 1}(1, 0, 0) times.
136 (144, 156, 158, 166){182, 186, 194, 206}(222, 224, 230) sts; 68 (72, 78, 79, 83){91, 93, 97, 103}(111, 112, 115) sts on both front and back. 19 (19, 19, 15, 15){19, 15, 15, 15}(19, 15, 15) sts between chart markers.

Work a further 5 (9, 5, 5, 5){5, 7, 7, 7}(11, 9, 7) rnds even. **128 (136, 148, 158, 166){174, 186, 194, 206} (214, 224, 230) sts**

Hip shaping

Next rnd [hip shaping rnd]: k5 (5, 5, 5, 6){6, 6, 6, 7}(7, 7, 7), M1, k to 5 (5, 5, 5, 6){6, 6, 6, 7}(7, 7, 7) sts before side-seam marker, M1, k5 (5, 5, 5, 6){6, 6, 6, 7}(7, 7, 7), sl m, k5 (5, 5, 5, 6){6, 6, 6, 7}(7, 7, 7), M1, k to 5 (5, 5, 5, 6){6, 6, 6, 7}(7, 7, 7) sts before beginning-of-rnd marker, M1, k5 (5, 5, 5, 6){6, 6, 6, 7}(7, 7, 7) to end of rnd.
132 (140, 152, 162, 170){178, 190, 198, 210}(218, 228, 234) sts; 66 (70, 76, 81, 85){89, 95, 99, 105} (109, 114, 117) sts on both front and back.

Continue as set, working a hip shaping inc rnd every 2 rnds a further 2 (2, 1, 1, 1){1, 1, 2, 2}(1, 1, 1) times, then every 4 rnds a further 2 (2, 3, 3, 3){3, 3, 2, 2}(3, 3, 3) times: on final inc rnd only, inc an additional 0 (0, 0, 1, 1){1, 1, 1, 1}(1, 0, 1) st at centre of back section and an additional 0 (0, 0, 1, 1){1, 1, 1, 1}(1, 0, 1) st at centre of front section.
148 (156, 168, 180, 188){196, 208, 216, 228}(236, 244, 252) sts; 74 (78, 84, 90, 94){98, 104, 108, 114} (118, 122, 126) on both front and back.

After final inc rnd, work 13 rnds even (or work until body is desired length before beginning ribbing), then break Yarn A and Yarn B and join in Yarn C; k 1 rnd, then switch to short circ smaller needles and work 11 rnds in k2, p2 rib. Cast off all sts using a stretchy cast-off.

SLEEVES

Make both alike
Beginning at centre of underarm cast-on, with RS facing and using DPNs (or needles for preferred method of working small circumferences in the round): join in Yarn A, pick up and k4 (4, 4, 4, 5){5, 6, 6, 6}(6, 7, 7) sts in underarm, sl 58 (57, 59, 57, 58){61, 65, 65, 67}(71, 73, 74) held sleeve sts back to needles, work across sleeve working Cable Chart Rnd 57 (59, 61, 63, 63){63, 67, 67, 69}(71, 73, 73), k to end of sleeve sts, pick up and k4 (5, 5, 4, 6){5, 6, 6, 6}(6, 8, 8) sts in underarm cast-on.

Next rnd: join in Yarn B, and continue as set (note that work will not technically be joined in the rnd until next rnd); for Sizes 4, 5 and 6 remove chart markers on this rnd.

64 (66, 64, 65, 69){71, 77, 77, 79}(83, 88, 89) sts; 11 (11, 12, 13, 15){16, 28, 28, 29}(31, 33, 34) sts before chart, 10 (12, 13, 13, 15){16, 28, 28, 29}(31, 34, 34) sts after chart. 43 (43, 39, 39, 39){39, 21, 21, 21}(21, 21, 21) sts between chart markers.

» All sizes
Sleeve Rnd 1: pm for beginning of rnd, join in Yarn A, k across rnd working from Cable Chart as set.

Continue as set for a further 7 rnds.

» Sizes 1-6 only:
When you reach Rnd 65, which will be on Sleeve Rnd 7 (5, 3, 1, 1) {1, -, -, -} (-, -, -), replace chart markers as follows: k20 (20, 21, 22, 24){25, -, -, -} (-, -, -), pm, work Cable Chart Rnd 65, pm, k19 (21, 22, 22, 24){25, -, -, -}(-, -, -), pm, work Cable Chart Rnd 65, pm, k to end of rnd.

» All sizes
Work a further 13 (15, 17, 19, 19){19, 19, 19, 19}(19, 19, 19) rnds even. **60 (62, 64, 65, 69){71, 77, 77, 79} (83, 88, 89) sts,** 21 sts between chart markers.

Sleeve shaping

Note that during the following sleeve shaping rounds the end of the Cable Chart will be reached; after completing Cable Chart Rnd 106, k the remaining 15 sts for the remainder of the sleeve (chart markers can either be removed at this point or left in place to help with counting stitches).

Next rnd [Sleeve Rnd 21 – sleeve shaping dec rnd]:
k1, k2tog, k to chart marker, work Cable Chart Rnd 79 (81, 83, 85, 85){85, 89, 89, 91}(93, 95, 95), k to 3 sts before end of rnd, ssk, k1.
58 **(60, 62, 63, 67){69, 75, 75, 77}(81, 86, 87) sts**
19 (19, 20, 21, 23){24, 27, 27, 28}(30, 32, 33) sts before chart, 18 (20, 21, 21, 23){24, 27, 27, 28}(30, 33, 33) sts after chart, 21 sts between chart markers.

Continue as set, working a sleeve shaping dec rnd every 8 (8, 8, 8, 8){8, 6, 6, 6}(6, 6, 6) rnds a further 10 (10, 9, 9, 4){7, 14, 14, 13}(13, 7, 7) times, then every 0 (6, 6, 6, 6){6, 4, 4, 4}(4, 4, 4) rnds a further 0 (1, 3, 3, 10){6, 2, 2, 4}(4, 13, 13) times: on final dec rnd only, dec an additional 0 (0, 0, 1, 1){1, 1, 1, 1}(1, 0, 1) st in centre of sleeve. 32 **(32, 32, 32, 32){36, 36, 36, 36}(40, 40, 40) sts**

Work a further 5 (1, 1, 1, 1){1, 3, 3, 1}(1, 1, 1) rnds even, or until sleeve is desired length before beginning cuff, then break Yarn A and Yarn B and join in Yarn C; k 1 rnd, then switch to smaller DPNs and work 11 rnds in k2, p2 rib. Cast off all sts using a stretchy cast-off.

FINISHING
Weave in all ends, and soak pullover according to yarn care instructions; carefully squeeze out excess moisture and lay out flat to dry completely.

CABLE CHART WRITTEN INSTRUCTONS

Rnd 1: k9, 1-into-5, k3, 1-into-5, k9. **31 sts**
Rnd 2: k9, sl2, p1, sl2, k3, sl2, p1, sl2, k9.
Rnd 3: k7, T4R[*el.*], *p1*, k7, p1, T4L[*el.*], k7.
Rnd 4: k7, sl2, p3, sl2, k1, 1-into-3, k1, sl2, p3, sl2, k7. **33 sts**
Rnd 5: k5, T4R[*el.*], p3, k2, T2R{*sl1*}, p1, T2L{*sl1*}, k2, p3, T4L[*el.*], k5.
Rnd 6: k5, sl2, p5, sl2, k1tbl[*el.*]1, p3, k1tbl[*el.*]1, sl2, p5, sl2, k5.
Rnd 7: k4, T3R, M1p, p5, C3L[*sl1, k2*], p3, C3L[*k2, sl1*], p5, M1p, T3L, k4. **35 sts**
Rnd 8: k4, sl2, p7, k1tbl[*el.*]1, sl2, p3, sl2, k1tbl[*el.*]1, p7, sl2, k4.
Rnd 9: k3, T3R, p5, T3R{*sl1*}, k2, p3, k2, T3L{*sl1*}, p5, T3L, k3.
Rnd 10: k3, sl2, p6, k1tbl[*el.*]1, p2, sl2, p3, sl2, p2, k1tbl[*el.*]1, p6, sl2, k3.
Rnd 11: k2, T3R, p4, T3R{*sl1*}, p2, k2, p3, k2, p2, T3L{*sl1*}, p4, T3L, k2.
Rnd 12: k2, sl2, p5, k1tbl, p4, sl2, p3, sl2, p4, k1tbl, p5, sl2, k2.
Rnd 13: k1, T3R, p4, T2R{*sl1*}, p4, k2, p3, k2, p4, T2L{*sl1*}, p4, T3L, k1.
Rnd 14: k1, sl2, p5, k1tbl, p5, sl2, p3, sl2, p5, k1tbl, p5, sl2, k1.
Rnd 15: T3R, p4, T2R{*sl1*}, p5, k2, p3, k2, p5, T2L{*sl1*}, p4, T3L.
Rnd 16: sl2, p5, k1tbl, p6, sl2, p3, sl2, p6, k1tbl, p5, sl2.
Rnd 17: k7, 1-into-5, T3R, p4, T2R{*sl1*}, p6, k2, p3, k2, p6, T2L{*sl1*}, p4, T3L, 1-into-5, k7. **61 sts**
Rnd 18: k7, sl2, pfbf, C4L{*sl4*}, p5, k1tbl, p7, sl2, p3, sl2, p7, k1tbl, p5, C4L{*sl4*}, pfbf, sl2,

CABLE CHART [Rnds 1–16]

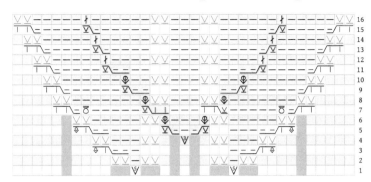

CHART KEY

For full Chart Key &
Abbreviations, see p. 73

k7. **65 sts**

Rnd 19: k3, k2tog, T4R[*dbl. el.*], M1p, p3, k2, T4L[*dbl. el.*], p2, T2R{*sl1*}, p7, k2, p3, k2, p7, T2L{*sl1*}, p2, T4R[*dbl. el.*], k2, p3, M1p, T4L[*dbl. el.*], ssk, k3.

Rnd 20: k1, k2tog, T3R{*sl2*}, M1p, p6, sl2, p2, T4L{*sl2*}, k1tbl, p8, sl2, p3, sl2, p8, k1tbl, T4R{*sl2*}, p2, sl2, p6, M1p, T3L{*sl2*}, ssk, k1.

Rnd 21: T4R[*el.*], p7, T3R, p4, C3R[*sl1, k2[el.]*], p7, T3R, p3, T3L, p7, C3R[*k2[el.]*], sl1, p4, T3L, p7, T4L[*el.*].

Rnd 22: sl2, p9, sl2, p5, k1tbl, T4L{*sl2*}, (p5, sl2) 2 times, p5, T4R{*sl2*}, k1tbl, p5, sl2, p9, sl2.

Rnd 23: k4, T3R, p9, k2, p4, T2R{*sl1*}, p2, T4L[*dbl. el.*], p2, T3R, p5, T3L, p2, T4R[*dbl. el.*], p2, T2L{*sl1*}, p4, k2, p9, T3L, k4. **75 sts**

Rnd 24: k4, sl2, p6, 1-into-3, p3, sl2, p4, k1tbl, p5, T4L{*sl2*}, sl2, p7, sl2, T4R{*sl2*}, p5, k1tbl, p4, sl2, p3, 1-into-3, p6, sl2, k4. **79 sts**

Rnd 25: k3, T3R, p6, sl1, p1, M1p, sl1, p2, T3R, p3, T2R{*sl1*}, p7, C4L[*el.*], p7, C4L[*el.*]{*k2*}, p7, T2L{*sl1*}, p3, T3L, p2, sl1, M1p, p1, sl1, p6, T3L, k3. **81 sts**

Rnd 26: k3, sl2, p7, k1tbl, p2, T3L[*p2, k1tbl[el.]*], sl2, p4, k1tbl, p8, sl4, p7, sl4, p8, k1tbl, p4, sl2, T3R[*k1tbl[el.], p2*], p2, k1tbl, p7, sl2, k3.

Rnd 27: k2, T3R, p7, sl1, p4, C3R[*k2, sl1*], p3, T2R{*sl1*}, p7, T3R, T4L[*el.*], p3, T4R[*el.*], T3L, p7, T2L{*sl1*}, p3, C3R[*sl1, k2*], p4, sl1, p7, T3L, k2.

Rnd 28: k2, sl2, p8, k1tbl, p4, sl2, T2L[*p1, k1tbl[el.]*], p2, k1tbl, p8, (sl2, p3) 3 times, sl2, p8, k1tbl, p2, T2R[*k1tbl[el.], p1*], sl2, p4, k1tbl, p8, sl2, k2.

Rnd 29: k1, T3R, p8, sl1, p4, k2, p1, T3L{*sl1*}, sl1, p7, T3R, p3, T3L, p1, T3R, p3, T3L, p7, sl1, T3R{*sl1*}, p1, k2, p4, sl1, p8, T3L, k1.

Rnd 30: k1, sl2, p9, k1tbl, p4, sl2, p3, C2L[*k1tbl, k1tbl[el.]*], p7, sl2, p5, sl2, p1, sl2, p5, sl2, p7, C2L[*k1tbl[el.]*], k1tbl], p3, sl2, p4, k1tbl, p9, sl2, k1.

Rnd 31: T3R, p9, sl1, p4, k2, p3, sl1, T4L{*sl1*}, p3, T3R, p5, C5R, p5, T3L, p3, T4R{*sl1*}, sl1, p3, k2, p4, sl1, p9, T3L.

Rnd 32: sl2, p10, k1tbl, p4, sl2, p3, k1tbl, p3, T4L[*p3, k1tbl[el.]*], sl2, p6, sl2, p1, sl2, p6, sl2, T4R[*k1tbl[el.]*], p3, p3, k1tbl, p3, sl2, p4, k1tbl, p10, sl2.

Rnd 33: C3L, p9, sl1, p4, k2, p3, sl1, p6, C3R[*k1[el.]*], k1, sl1], p4, T4R, p1, T4L, p4, C3R[*sl1, k1, k1[el.]*], p6, sl1, p3, k2, p4, sl1, p9, C3R.

Rnd 34: k1, sl2, k3, p6, k1tbl, p4, sl2, p3, k1tbl, p4, T4R{*sl2*}, T3L[*p2, k1[el.]*tbl], p2, sl2, p5, sl2, p2, T3R[*k1[el.]*tbl, *p2*], T4L{*sl2*}, p4, k1tbl, p3, sl2, p4, k1tbl, p6, k3, sl2, k1.

Rnd 35: k1, C5L[*dbl. el.*], k3, p3, sl1, p4, k2, p3, T2L[*p1, sl1*], T5R[*dbl. el.*], p4, T2L[*p1, sl1*], T3R, p5, T3L, T2R[*sl1, p1*], p4, T5L[*dbl. el.*], T2R[*sl1, p1*], p3, k2, p4, sl1, p3, k3, C5R[*dbl. el.*], k1.

Rnd 36: k4, C5L{*sl2*}, k3, k1tbl, p4, sl2, p4, C3L[*sl2, k1tbl*], p8, k1tbl, sl2, p7, sl2, k1tbl, p8, C3L[*k1tbl, sl2*], p4, sl2, p4, k1tbl, k3, C5R{*sl2*}, k4.

Rnd 37: k5, ssk, C5L[*dbl. el.*], sl1, p4, k2, p2, T4R[*dbl. el.*], sl1, p8, C3L[*k2, sl1*], p7, C3L[*sl1, k2*], p8, sl1, T4L[*dbl. el.*], p2, k2, p4, sl1, C5R[*dbl. el.*], k2tog, k5. **79 sts**

Rnd 38: k9, C3R[*k1tbl, sl2*], p4, sl2, T4R{*sl2*}, p2, k1tbl, p8, sl2, k1tbl, p7, k1tbl, sl2, p8, k1tbl, p2, T4L{*sl2*}, sl2, p4, C3R{*sl2, k1tbl*}, k9.

Rnd 39: k7, ssk, sl1, T5L[*el.*], *p1*, C4R[*el.*], p4, T2L{*sl1*}, p6, T3R, T2L{*sl1*}, p5, T2R{*sl1*}, T3L, p6, T2R{*sl1*}, p4, C4R{*k2*}[*el.*], *p1*, T5R[*el.*], sl1, k2tog, k7. **77 sts**

Rnd 40: k8, k1 tbl, p1, ssp, 5-into-1[*p*], sl2, p5, k1tbl, p6, sl2, p2, k1 tbl, p5, k1tbl, p2, sl2, p6, k1 tbl, p5, sl2, 5-into-1[*p*], p2tog, p1, k1 tbl, k8. **67 sts**

Rnd 41: sl1, p3, T3L, p4, T3L{*sl1*}, p3, T3R,

p2, sl1, p5, sl1, p2, T3L, p3, T3R{*sl1*}, p4, T3R, p3, sl1. **51 sts**

Rnd 42: k1tbl, p4, sl2, p6, k1tbl[*el.*]1, p3, sl2, p3, k1tbl, p5, k1tbl, p3, sl2, p3, k1tbl[*el.*]1, p6, sl2, p4, k1tbl.

Rnd 43: C2L{*sl1*}, p3, T3L, p5, T3L{*sl1*}, T3R, p3, T2L{*sl1*}, p3, T2R{*sl1*}, p3, T3L, T3R{*sl1*}, p5, T3R, p3, C2R{*sl1*}.

Rnd 44: k1, k1tbl, p4, sl2, p7, k1tbl[*el.*]1, sl2, p5, k1tbl, p3, k1tbl, p5, sl2, k1tbl[*el.*]1, p7, sl2, p4, k1tbl, k1.

Rnd 45: k1, C2L{*sl1*}, p3, T3L, p6, C3R[*k2, sl1*], p5, sl1, p3, sl1, p5, C3R[*sl1, k2*], p6, T3R, p3, C2R{*sl1*}, k1.

Rnd 46: k2, k1tbl, p4, sl2, p6, sl2, k1tbl[*el.*]1, p5, k1tbl, p3, k1tbl, p5, k1tbl[*el.*]1, sl2, p6, sl2, p4, k1tbl, k2.

Rnd 47: k2, C2L{*sl1*}, p3, T3L, p5, k2, T3L{*sl1*}, (p3, sl1) 2 times, p3, T3R{*sl1*}, k2, p5, T3R, p3, C2R{*sl1*}, k2.

Rnd 48: k3, k1tbl, p4, sl2, p5, sl2, p2, k1tbl[*el.*]1, (p3, k1tbl) 2 times, p3, k1tbl[*el.*]1, p2, sl2, p5, sl2, p4, k1tbl, k3.

Rnd 49: k3, C2L{*sl1*}, p3, T4L[*el.*], p2, T3R, p2, T3L{*sl1*}, p1, sl1, p3, sl1, p1, T3R{*sl1*}, p2, T3L, p2, T4R[*el.*], p3, C2R{*sl1*}, k3.

Rnd 50: k4, k1tbl, p5, sl2, p2, sl2, p5, 3-into-1[*p*], p3, 3-into-1[*p*], p5, sl2, p2, sl2, p5, k1tbl, k4. **47 sts**

Rnd 51: k4, C2L{*sl1*}, p4, T4L[*el.*], k2, p15, k2, T4R[*el.*], p4, C2R{*sl1*}, k4.

Rnd 52: k5, k1tbl, p6, sl4, p15, sl4, p6, k1tbl, k5.

Rnd 53: k5, C2L{*sl1*}, p5, C4L, p15, C4L, p5, C2R{*sl1*}, k5.

Rnd 54: k6, k1tbl, p5, sl4, p6, p2sl1psso, p6,

CHART NOTES

Note that, due to the width of the chart, Rnds 23—40 of the Cable Chart have been split in half. To work from this chart, work from the first half and then the second half of each rnd (the black line down the edges of each half show where the chart has been split).

CABLE CHART [Rnds 17—22]

CABLE CHART [Rnds 23—40] (FIRST HALF)

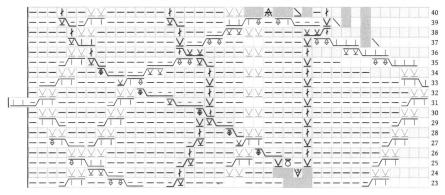

CABLE CHART [Rnds 23—40] (SECOND HALF)

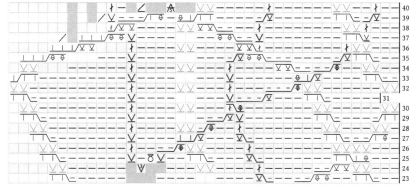

sl4, p5, k1tbl, k6. **45 sts**

Rnd 55: k6, C2L{*sl1*}, p4, k2, T3L, p11, T3R, k2, p4, C2R{*sl1*}, k6.

Rnd 56: k7, k1tbl, p4, sl2, p1, sl2, p11, sl2, p1, sl2, p4, k1tbl, k7.

Rnd 57: k7, C2L{*sl1*}, ssp, T3R, p1, T3L, p9, T3R, p1, T3L, p2tog, C2R{*sl1*}, k7. **43 sts**

Rnd 58: k8, k1tbl[*el.*]1, p1, sl2, p3, sl2, p9, sl2, p3, sl2, p1, k1tbl[*el.*]1, k8.

Rnd 59: k8, C2L{*sl1*}, k2, p3, T4L[*el.*], p5, T4R[*el.*], p3, k2, C2R{*sl1*}, k8.

Rnd 60: k9, k1tbl[*el.*]1, (sl2, p5) 3 times, sl2, k1tbl[*el.*]1, k9.

Rnd 61: k9, C3R[*k2, sl1*], p5, T4L[*el.*], *p1*, T4R[*el.*], p5, C3R[*sl1, k2*], k9.

Rnd 62: k9, sl2, k1tbl[*el.*]1, p7, 5-into-1[*p*], p7, k1tbl[*el.*]1, sl2, k9. **39 sts**

Rnd 63: k11, T3L{*sl1*}, p11, T3R{*sl1*}, k11.

Rnd 64: k9, sl2, p2, k1tbl[*el.*]1, p11, k1tbl[*el.*]1, p2, sl2, k9

Rnd 65: k2, p2, T3L{*sl1*}, p7, T3R{*sl1*}, p2, k2. **21 sts**

Rnd 66: sl2, p4, k1tbl[*el.*]1, p7, k1tbl[*el.*]1, p4, sl2.

Rnd 67: C3L, p3, T3L{*sl1*}, p3, T3R{*sl1*}, p3, C3R.

Rnd 68: k1, sl2, p5, k1tbl[*el.*]1, p3, k1tbl[*el.*]1, p5, sl2, k1.

Rnd 69: k3, p5, T2L{*sl1*}, p1, T2R{*sl1*}, p5, k3.

Rnd 70: k1, sl2, p6, k1tbl, p1, k1tbl, p6, sl2, k1.

Rnd 71: k1, C3L, p5, C3L[*sl1, p1, sl1*], p5, C3R, k1.

Rnd 72: k2, sl2, p5, k1tbl, p1, k1tbl, p5, sl2, k2.

Rnd 73: k4, p3, T3R{*sl1*}, p1, T3L{*sl1*}, p3, k4.

Rnd 74: k2, sl2, p3, k1tbl[*el.*]1, p5, k1tbl[*el.*]1, p3, sl2, k2.

Rnd 75: k2, C3L, T3R{*sl1*}, p5, T3L{*sl1*}, C3R, k2.

Rnd 76: k3, sl2, k1tbl[*el.*]1, p9, k1tbl[*el.*]1, sl2, k3.

CABLE CHART [Rnds 41–64]

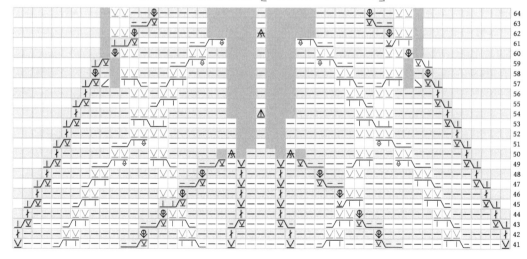

CABLE CHART [Rnds 65–106]

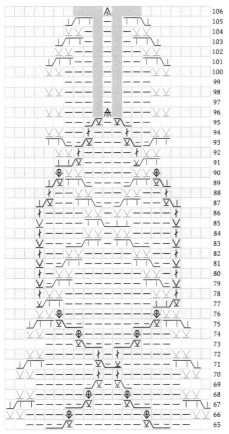

Rnd 77: k3, C3R[*sl1, k2*], p9, C3R[*k2, sl1*], k3.

Rnd 78: k3, k1tbl, sl2, p9, sl2, k1tbl, k3.

Rnd 79: k3, sl1, T3L, p7, T3R, sl1, k3.

Rnd 80: k3, k1tbl, p1, sl2, p7, sl2, p1, k1tbl, k3.

Rnd 81: k3, sl1, p1, T3L, p5, T3R, p1, sl1, k3.

Rnd 82: k3, k1tbl, p2, sl2, p5, sl2, p2, k1tbl, k3.

Rnd 83: k3, sl1, p2, T4L, p1, T4R, p2, sl1, k3.

Rnd 84: k3, k1tbl, p4, sl2, p1, sl2, p4, k1tbl, k3.

Rnd 85: k3, sl1, p4, C5L, p4, sl1, k3. **21 sts**

Rnd 86: k3, k1tbl, p4, sl2, p1, sl2, p4, k1tbl, k3.

Rnd 87: k3, C2L{*sl1*}, p2, T3R, p1, T3L, p2, C2R{*sl1*}, k3.

Rnd 88: k4, k1tbl, p2, sl2, p3, sl2, p2, k1tbl, k4.

Rnd 89: k4, C2L{*sl1*}, T3R, p3, T3L, C2R{*sl1*}, k4.

Rnd 90: k5, k1tbl[*el.*]1, sl2, p5, sl2, k1tbl[*el.*]1, k5.

Rnd 91: k5, C3R[*k2, sl1*], p5, C3R[*sl1, k2*], k5.

Rnd 92: k5, sl2, k1tbl, p5, k1tbl, sl2, k5.

Rnd 93: k4, T3R, T2L{*sl1*}, p3, T2R{*sl1*}, T3L, k4.

Rnd 94: k4, sl2, p2, k1tbl, p3, k1tbl, p2, sl2, k4.

Rnd 95: k6, p2, T2L{*sl1*}, p1, T2R{*sl1*}, p2, k6.

Rnd 96: k4, sl2, p3, 3-into-1[*p*], p3, sl2, k4. **19 sts**

Rnd 97: k6, p7, k6.

Rnd 98: k4, sl2, p7, sl2, k4.

Rnd 99: k6, p7, k6.

Rnd 100: repeat Rnd 98.

Rnd 101: k4, C3L, p5, C3R, k4.

Rnd 102: k5, sl2, p5, sl2, k5.

Rnd 103: k5, C3L, p3, C3R, k5.

Rnd 104: k6, sl2, p3, sl2, k6.

Rnd 105: k6, C3L, p1, C3R, k6.

Rnd 106: k7, 5-into-1, k7. **15 sts**

CHART KEY & ABBREVIATIONS

ELONGATED STITCHES

All of the patterns in this book make use of elongated cable stitches, in which the yarn is wrapped twice in one or two stitches to provide extra stretch in areas where the cable is travelling nearly horizontally. When working into these stitches on the following round, treat each double-wrapped stitch as a single stitch - insert your needle into one of the wraps and let the other wrap simply slip off the needle. In all stitch counts, any double-wrapped stitches are counted as 1 stitch.

Elongated stitches may be worked on their own, or (more commonly) as part of a cable; in written instructions, they are indicated by the suffix [*el.*] or [*dbl. el.*], and in charts by the symbol: ⬦

HOW TO USE THIS SECTION

General abbreviations used throughout this book are listed under **Standard Abbreviations** (p. 74).

General chart key symbols (all single square) are listed under **General Chart Key** (p. 75).

All cable stitches, and special stitches that are used in combination with cable stitches, are listed under **Special Abbreviations & Cable Symbols** (p. 75).

The Special Abbreviations & Cable Symbols section is arranged alphabetically using the prefix at the beginning of each cable stitch (for example, all C4L stitches are grouped together, all T3R stitches are grouped together, etc.), however within each group of stitches with the same prefix the entries are arranged not alphabetically but by the similarity of the execution of the stitch.

CHART CONVENTIONS

All charts show the work as it appears from the right side; when working in the round, each round should be read from the right to the left. White squares of the chart indicate the main colour Yarn A and light grey squares indicate the background colour (Yarn B, C or D); this is intended as a reminder to change colours on each round

FURTHER INFORMATION

For further information and help regarding the techniques used in this book, please visit: **www.lucyhague.co.uk/tutorials**

To download a PDF version of the Chart Key & Abbreviations, which you can print out to have on hand whilst working from the patterns, please visit: **www.lucyhague.co.uk/illuminated-knits**

The prefixes for the cable stitches generally follow the system briefly described below, with extra details contained in square or curly brackets if necessary.

Examples of cable stitch names:

C4L

C - usually two cable strands crossing over each other (occasionally one strand crossing over background)

4 - number of stitches involved

L - direction of cross (left)

T3R

T - usually one cable strand crossing over background

3 - number of stitches involved

R - direction of cross (right)

STANDARD ABBREVIATIONS

cn/ln/rn	cable needle/left needle/right needle
dec/dec'g	decrease/decreasing (any method can be used to decrease 1 st, such as k2tog)
DPN	double-pointed needle
inc/inc'g	increase/increasing (any method can be used to increase 1 k st, such as M1)
k	knit
k2sl1psso	k2tog, sl st to ln, pass second st on ln over st just slipped, sl st back to rn
k2tog	k 2 sts tog
kfb	k into front, then back, of same st
kfbf	k into front, then back, then front of st
M1	make 1 k st
M1p	make 1 p st
p	purl
p2sl1psso	p2tog, sl st to ln wyif, pass second st on ln over st just slipped, sl st back to rn
p2tog	p 2 sts tog
p3tog	p 3 sts tog
pfb	purl into front, then back of same st
pfbf	p into front, then back, then front of st

(p)m	(place) marker
rem	remaining
rep	repeat
rnd	round
RS/WS	right side/wrong side
sl	slip (purlwise)
sl1k2psso	sl 1 st, k2tog, pass slipped st over st just worked
ssk	sl 2 sts knitwise, separately, then sl sts back to left needle and k 2 sts tog tbl
ssp	sl 2 st knitwise, separately, then sl sts back to left needle and p 2 sts tog tbl
sssp	sl 3 sts knitwise, separately, then sl sts back to left needle and p 3 sts tog tbl
st(s)	stitch(es)
tbl	through back of loop
tog	together
w&t	wrap and turn (for short row): wyif, sl 1 st from ln to rn, purlwise; bring yarn to back, turn work
wyib/wyif	with yarn in back/with yarn in front
yo	yarn over

ILLUMINATED KNITS | *Lucy Hague*

GENERAL CHART KEY

☐ RS: k WS: p	V RS: sl wyib WS: sl wyif	/ k2tog	▲ RS: p2sl1psso WS: sl1k2psso
☐ light grey background indicates st is worked with Yarn B	⊬ kfb	\ ssk	
	⩔ kfbf	∠ RS: p2tog WS: k2tog	⚡ p2tog with 1 st from circ needle
— RS: p WS: k	⩊ pfb	⊿ p3tog	⚔ p3tog with 2 sts from circ needle
▨ No stitch	⩡ pfbf	⟍ RS: ssp WS: ssk	○ yo
▦ see Chart Notes	ర M1	⟑ sssp	
	ठ M1p		

SPECIAL ABBREVIATIONS & CABLE SYMBOLS

1-into-3	ⱽ₃	insert rn between first 2 sts on ln, wrap yarn and pull through, sl first st on ln to rn; insert ln between first 2 sts on rn, wrap yarn around ln as though to make k st, pull yarn through, sl st just created to rn. 1 st increased to 3 sts
1-into-5	ⱽ₅	*insert rn between first 2 sts on ln, wrap yarn and pull through, sl first st on ln to rn; insert ln between first 2 sts on rn, wrap yarn around ln as though to make k st, pull yarn through*, sl first st on rn back to ln. Repeat instructions between asterisks once more, sl st just created to rn, sl rem sts on ln to rn. 1 st increased to 5 sts
1-into-7	ⱽ	as for 1-into-5, but repeat instructions between asterisks one extra time, sl st just created to rn, sl rem sts on ln to rn. 1 st increased to 7 sts
3-into-1	⩓₃	sl next 2 sts to rn, pass 2nd slipped st over first st on rn and off needle. Pass st from rn back to ln and slip 2nd st on ln over first st and off needle; k rem st. 3 sts decreased to 1 st
3-into-1[p]	⩓₃	as for 3-into-1 but p rem st
3-into-1[sl]	⩓₃	as for 3-into-1 but sl rem st wyif

5-into-1	$\triangle$	sl next 3 sts to rn, pass second slipped st over first st on rn and off needle. sl st from rn back to ln and pass second st on ln over first st and off needle. sl st from ln to rn and pass second st over first st and off needle. sl rem st on rn back to ln and pass second st on ln over first st and off needle; k rem st. 5 sts decreased to 1 st
5-into-1[*p*]	$\triangle$	on RS - as 5-into-1 but p rem st; on WS - as 5-into-1
C2L[*k1tbl, k1tbl[el.]*]		sl next st to cn and hold to front; k1tbl, k1tbl[el.] from cn
C2L[*k1tbl[el.], k1tbl*]		sl next st to cn and hold to front; k1tbl[el.], k1tbl from cn
C2L{*sl1*}		sl next st to cn and hold to front; k1, sl1 from cn
C2L{*sl2*}		sl next st to cn and hold to front; sl1, sl1 from cn
C2R{*sl1*}		sl next st to cn and hold to back; sl1, k1 from cn
C2R{*sl2*}		sl next st to cn and hold to back; sl1, sl1 from cn
C3L		sl next 2 sts to cn and hold to front; k1, k2 from cn
C3L[*sl1, k2*]		sl next 2 sts to cn and hold to front; sl1, k2 from cn
C3L{*sl2*}		sl next 2 sts to cn and hold to front; k1, sl2 from cn
C3L[*k1tbl, sl2*]		sl next 2 sts to cn and hold to front; k1tbl, sl2 from cn
C3L[*k2, sl1*]		sl next st to cn and hold to front; k2, sl1 from cn
C3L[*sl1, p1, sl1*]		sl next 2 sts to cn and hold to front; sl1 from ln, sl left-most st from cn back to ln and p1, sl1 from cn
C3L[*sl2, k1tbl*]		sl next st to cn and hold to front; sl2, k1tbl from cn
C3R		sl next st to cn and hold to back; k2, k1 from cn

C3R[*k2, sl1*]	⊻/⊺⊺	sl next st to cn and hold to back; k2, sl1 from cn
C3R[*k1[el.], k1, sl1*]	⊻/⊺♀	sl next st to cn and hold to back; k1 wrapping yarn twice rnd needle, k1, sl1 from cn
C3R[*k2[el.], sl1*]	⊻/♀♀	sl next st to cn and hold to back; [k1 wrapping yarn twice rnd needle] twice, sl1 from cn
C3R{*sl2*}	⊺/⊻⊻	sl next st to cn and hold to back; sl2, k1 from cn
C3R[*sl2, k1tbl*]	ⱦ/⊻⊻	sl next st to cn and hold to back; sl2, k1tbl from cn
C3R[*sl1, k2*]	⊺⊺/⊻	sl next 2 sts to cn and hold to back; sl1, k2 from cn
C3R[*sl1, k1, k1[el.]*]	♀⊺/⊻	sl next 2 sts to cn and hold to back; sl1, [k1, k1 wrapping yarn twice rnd needle] from cn
C3R[*sl1, k2[el.]*]	♀♀/⊻	sl next 2 sts to cn and hold to back; sl1, [k1 wrapping yarn twice rnd needle] twice from cn
C3R[*sl1, p1, sl1*]	⊻ –/⊻	sl next 2 sts to cn and hold to back; sl1 from ln; sl leftmost st on cn to ln and bring cn to front; p1 from ln, sl1 from cn
C3R[*k1tbl, sl2*]	⊻ ⊻/ⱦ	sl next 2 sts to cn and hold to back; k1tbl, sl2 from cn
C4L	⊺ ⊺\⊺ ⊺	sl next 2 sts to cn and hold to front; k2, k2 from cn
C4L[*el.*]	♀ ⊺\⊺ ⊺	sl next 2 sts to cn and hold to front; k2, [k1, k1 wrapping yarn twice rnd needle] from cn
C4L[*dbl. el.*]	♀ ♀\⊺ ⊺	sl next 2 sts to cn and hold to front; k2, [k1 wrapping yarn twice rnd needle] twice from cn
C4L[*el.*]{*k2*}	⊺ ⊺\⊺ ♀	sl next 2 sts to cn and hold to front; k1 wrapping yarn twice rnd needle, k1, k2 from cn

C4L[*dbl. el.*]{*k2*} `T T\⚇ ⚇` sl next 2 sts to cn and hold to front; [{k1 wrapping yarn twice rnd needle} twice], k2 from cn

C4L[*sl2*]{*k2*} `T T\∨ ∨` sl next 2 sts to cn and hold to front; sl2, k2 from cn

C4L{*sl2*} `∨ ∨\| |` on RS - sl next 2 sts to cn and hold to front; k2, sl2 from cn; on WS - sl next 2 sts to cn and hold to front; sl2, p2 from cn

C4L{*sl4*} `∨ ∨\∨ ∨` sl next 2 sts to cn and hold to front; sl2, sl2 from cn

C4L[*T2R{sl1}*] `T T\ _/∨` sl next 2 sts to cn and hold to front; sl next 2 sts from ln to rn; sl 1st st on rn to cn, sl next st on rn back to ln; sl1 from cn, p1 from ln, k2 from cn

C4L{*dbl.el*}[*T2R{sl1}*] `⚇ ⚇\ _/∨` sl next 2 sts to cn and hold to front; sl next 2 sts from ln to rn; sl 1st st on rn to cn, sl next st on rn back to ln; sl1 from cn, p1 from ln, [k1 wrapping yarn twice rnd needle] twice from cn

C4L{*sl1*}[*T3R*] `∨\ _/T T` sl next st to cn and hold to front; sl next 3 sts from ln to rn; sl first 2 sts on rn to cn; sl next st on rn to ln; k2 from cn, p1 from ln, sl1 from cn

C4L{*sl1*}[*T3R{dbl. el.}*] `∨\ _/⚇ ⚇` sl next st to cn and hold to front; sl next 3 sts from ln to rn; sl first 2 sts on rn to cn; sl next st on rn to ln; [k1 wrapping yarn twice rnd needle] twice from cn, p1 from ln, sl1 from cn

C4R `| |/T T` sl next 2 sts to cn and hold to back; k2, k2 from cn

C4R[*el.*] `| |/T ⚇` sl next 2 sts to cn and hold to back; k1 wrapping yarn twice rnd needle, k1, k2 from cn

C4R[*dbl. el.*] `| |/⚇ ⚇` on RS - sl next 2 sts to cn and hold to back; [{k1 wrapping yarn twice rnd needle} twice], k2 from cn; on WS - sl next 2 sts to cn and hold to back; p2, [{p1 wrapping yarn twice rnd needle} twice] from cn

C4R{*k2*}[*el.*] `⚇ |/T T` sl next 2 sts to cn and hold to back; k2, [k1, k1 wrapping yarn twice rnd needle] from cn

C4R{*k2*}[*dbl. el.*] ⊻ ⊻/⊤ ⊤   on RS - sl next 2 sts to cn and hold to back; k2, [{k1 wrapping yarn twice rnd needle} twice] from cn; on WS - sl next 2 sts to cn and hold to back; [{p1 wrapping yarn twice rnd needle} twice], p2 from cn

C4R{*k2*}[*sl2*] ⋁ ⋁/⊤ ⊤   sl next 2 sts to cn and hold to back; k2, sl2 from cn

C4R{*sl2*} ⊥ ⊥/⋁ ⋁   on RS - sl next 2 sts to cn and hold to back; sl2, k2 from cn; on WS - sl next 2 sts to cn and hold to back; p2, sl2 from cn

C4R[*T2L{sl1}*] ⋁−/⊤ ⊤   sl next 2 sts to cn and hold to back; k2 from ln, sl leftmost st on cn to ln and hold cn to front; p1 from ln, sl1 from cn

C4R{*sl1*}[*T3L*] ⊤⊤−/⋁   sl next 3 sts to cn and hold to back; sl next st from ln to rn; sl leftmost st on cn to ln and hold cn to front; p1 from ln, k2 from cn

C5L ⊤⊤\−⊥⊥   sl next 3 sts to cn and hold to front; k2, sl left-most st from cn back to ln and p1, k2 from cn

C5L[*dbl. el.*] ⊻ ⊻\⊥⊥⊥   sl next 2 sts to cn and hold to front; k3, [{k1 wrapping yarn twice rnd needle} twice] from cn

C5L{*sl2*} ⋁ ⋁\⊥⊥⊥   sl next 2 sts to cn and hold to front; k3, sl2 from cn

C5R ⊥⊥−/⊤⊤   sl next 3 sts to cn and hold to back; k2, sl left-most st from cn back to ln and p1, k2 from cn

C5R[*dbl. el.*] ⊥⊥⊥/⊻ ⊻   sl next 3 sts to cn and hold to back; [{k1 wrapping yarn twice rnd needle} twice], k3 from cn

C5R{*sl2*} ⊥⊥⊥/⋁ ⋁   sl next 3 sts to cn and hold to back; sl2, k3 from cn

k1[*el.*] ⊻   k1 wrapping twice rnd needle (this double-wrapped stitch is counted as one stitch; on next rnd, insert rn into one of the wraps to work and let other wrap slip off ln)

k1tbl[*el.*] ⊕   as for k1[el.] but k tbl

T2L[*p1, k1tbl[el.]*]	⏷\ −	sl next st to cn and hold to front; p1, [k1tbl wrapping yarn twice rnd needle] from cn
T2L{*sl1*}	∨\ −	sl next st to cn and hold to front; p1, sl1 from cn
T2R[*k1tbl[el.], p1*]	− /⏷	sl next st to cn and hold to back; k1tbl wrapping yarn twice rnd needle, p1 from cn
T2R{*sl1*}	− /∨	sl next st to cn and hold to back; sl1, p1 from cn
T3L	⊤ ⊤\ −	on RS - sl next 2 sts to cn and hold to front; p1, k2 from cn; on WS - sl next st to cn and hold to front; p2, k1 from cn
T3L{*sl2*}	∨ ∨\ −	sl next 2 sts to cn and hold to front; p1, sl2 from cn
T3L[*p2, k1tbl[el.]*]	⏷\ − −	sl next st to cn and hold to front; p2, k1tbl[el.] from cn
T3L{*sl1*}	∨\ − −	sl next st to cn and hold to front; p2, sl1 from cn
T3R	− /⊤ ⊤	on RS - sl next st to cn and hold to back; k2, p1 from cn; on WS - sl next 2 sts to cn and hold to back; k1, p2 from cn
T3R{*sl2*}	− /∨ ∨	sl next st to cn and hold to back; sl2, p1 from cn
T3R[*k1tbl[el.], p2*]	− − /⏷	sl next 2 sts to cn and hold to back; k1tbl[el.], p2 from cn
T3R{*sl1*}	− − /∨	sl next 2 sts to cn and hold to back; sl1, p2 from cn
T4L	⊤ ⊤\ − −	on RS - sl next 2 sts to cn and hold to front; p2, k2 from cn; on WS - as for RS
T4L[*el.*]	⏷ ⊤\ − −	on RS - sl next 2 sts to cn and hold to front; p2, [k1, k1 wrapping yarn twice rnd needle] from cn; on WS - sl next 2 sts to cn and hold to front; [p1 wrapping yarn twice rnd needle, p1], k2 from cn
T4L[*dbl. el.*]	⏷ ⏷\ − −	sl next 2 sts to cn and hold to front; p2, [{k1 wrapping yarn twice rnd needle} twice] from cn

T4L{*sl2*}	▽ ▽\– –	sl next 2 sts to cn and hold to front; p2, sl2 from cn
T4L[*p3, k1tbl[el.]*]	⊕\– – –	sl next st to cn and hold to front; p3, k1tbl[el.] from cn
T4L{*sl1*}	▽\– – –	sl next st to cn and hold to front; p3, sl1 from cn
T4R	– –/⊤ ⊤	on RS - sl next 2 sts to cn and hold to back; k2, p2 from cn; on WS - as for RS
T4R[*el.*]	– –/⊤ ⊕	on RS - sl next 2 sts to cn and hold to back; [k1, k1 wrapping yarn twice rnd needle], p2 from cn; on WS - sl next 2 sts to cn and hold to back; k2, [p1, p1 wrapping yarn twice rnd needle] from cn
T4R[*dbl. el.*]	– –/⊕ ⊕	sl next 2 sts to cn and hold to back; [{k1 wrapping yarn twice rnd needle} twice], p2 from cn
T4R{*sl2*}	– –/▽ ▽	sl next 2 sts to cn and hold to back; sl2, p2 from cn
T4R[*k1tbl[el.], p3*]	– – –/⊕	sl next 3 sts to cn and hold to back; k1tbl[el.], p3 from cn
T4R{*sl1*}	– – –/▽	sl next 3 sts to cn and hold to back; sl1, p3 from cn
T5L[*el.*]	⊕ ⊤\– – –	sl next 2 sts to cn and hold to front; p3, [k1, k1 wrapping yarn twice rnd needle] from cn
T5L[*dbl. el.*]	⊕ ⊕\– – –	sl next 2 sts to cn and hold to front; p3, [{k1 wrapping yarn twice rnd needle} twice] from cn
T5L{*sl2*}	▽ ▽\– – –	sl next 2 sts to cn and hold to front; p3, sl2 from cn
T5R[*el.*]	– – –/⊤ ⊕	sl next 3 sts to cn and hold to back; [k1, k1 wrapping yarn twice rnd needle], p3 from cn
T5R[*dbl. el.*]	– – –/⊕ ⊕	sl next 3 sts to cn and hold to back; [{k1 wrapping yarn twice rnd needle} twice], p3 from cn
T5R{*sl2*}	– – –/▽ ▽	sl next 3 sts to cn and hold to back; sl2, p3 from cn

To access PDF versions of these diagrams, which can be coloured in to try out different colour combinatons, visit:

www.lucyhague.co.uk/illuminated-knits

Lightning Source UK Ltd.
Milton Keynes UK
UKRC011241191218
334236UK00007B/108

* 9 7 8 0 9 9 2 7 6 9 0 1 7 *